Broadcasting Education

DPH Education Series

Broadcasting Education

U K SINGH • K N SUDARSHAN

DISCOVERY PUBLISHING HOUSE
NEW DELHI-110002

Published by:
Tilak Wasan

DISCOVERY PUBLISHING HOUSE PVT. LTD.
4383/4B, Ansari Road, Darya Ganj
New Delhi-110 002 (India)
Phone : +91-11-23279245, 23253475, 43596065
E-mail : discoverypublishinghouse@gmail.com
sales@discoverypublishinggroup.com
web : www.discoverypublishinggroup.com

Edition: **2020**

ISBN: 978-81-7141-368-3

Broadcasting Education

Printed at:
Infinity Imaging Systems
Delhi

Preface

The *DPH Education Handbook* has been created to provide access to information about contemporary topics in education. Practitioners and students at all levels in education have a need to know what is happening today, in addition to historical treatments within the literature.

Each chapter within the Handbook is designed to provide the user with needed "state-of-the-art" information as well as further sources of information. One of the significant features of each chapter is the inclusion of specific programmes, projects and activities so that the researcher can locate human resources as well as the literature.

The handbook will be of use to graduate and post graduate students in education and to practicing teachers, administrators, librarians and planners. The chapters and the further sources of information cited in each book should lead the reader to thousands of people and documents for either research or programme planning purposes.

An effort to achieve universal and effective education is based on a recognition of the rights of students to basic education that enables them to thrive in a complex society, as well as a realization the technological and economic growth is facilitated by increasing the numbers of students, even those with poor academic progresses, who are, in fact successful in learning. Thus, recent and current efforts improve education serve both private and social interests.

This series is addressed to administrators, planners and educators working in the field of education and training with a view to stimulating interest and attention in the areas of education and its related fields. It is also addressed to a growing number of teachers and instructors who will be practitioners in education and who will need to be acquainted with the modern aspects of educational practice and development. Many ideas, generalisations and discussions presented in this series should also prove useful to employing organisations committed to provide training facilities within their establishments—leading to effective mutual participation by institutions and organisations.

The editors wishes to thank the contributors, as well as those organizations that gave permission to publish their extracts, chapters etc.

Editors

Contents

1

The Impact of New Technology on Broadcasting Education

For the last twenty years, educational broadcasting in Britain has enjoyed a relatively stable and comfortable existence. That security and tranquaillity is quite suddenly being shattered as a result of major technological and political developments. New information technology is going to change educational broadcasting in ways that were inconceivable only five years ago. What exactly these changes will be is not easy to predict, but fundamental changes there certainly will be.

Radio and cassettes

A great deal of publicity is being given to high technology in education, particularly microcomputers and video-discs. There is a away from the effects of equally powerful low-cost technology. Audio recording is not new in education, nor glamorous, but the development of cheap, easy-to-use audio-cassette equipment has already had a major impact on the use of educational broadcasting, both in schools and adult education.

For many years, schools have used tape-records to record school radio broadcasts. Nearly all schools now hav、 audio recording equipment. Recording is ubiquitous, and the ability to record has been much enhanced by the introduction of combined radio-cassette machines. Recording became even more significant in 1983 when the BBC switched secondary school radio broadcasts from afternoon to night-time transmission. This move, resulting from the wish of the BBC Radio 4 Controller to offer popular programmes to a wider audience on the VHF (FM) band-width, requires recordings to be made in schools automatically at night-time using time-switches. This change has been implemented despite initial opposition from the BBC's own Educational schools had electronic time-switches, and night-time transmission requires local education authorities to spend over 200,000 on extra equipment. It entails centralised planning of recordings in advance and a pilot showed that there was a high failure rate in overnight recording due to teachers not correctly operating the automatic recording equipment. The BBC radio producers, the Educational Broadcasting Council and the local education authorities all thought that the move would reduce the use of radio in secondary schools. At the time of writing, it is not known whether these predictions will come true. However, in Norway and Sweden, an alternative system works very effectively. Most local education authorities have set up an audio-visual unit in vision programmes are recorded off-air by a full time technician in which they request the programmes that they need. The service is relatively cheap to run and there is virtually no failure rate in there is no real need to broadcast radio at all since all programmes could be mailed on tape at very low cost to the local centres.

At the Open University, the impact of audio-cassettes on radio has been dramatic, with radio transmission in 1983 dropping to less than thirteen hours a week, and over 500,000 cassettes being mailed to students. Furthermore, more than a third of the students who listen to the radio programmes that remain do so on recordings. In 1982 91 per cent of Open University students had audio-cassette players. Just under half of the radio recordings are made off-air by students themselves but the majority are heard from cassette tapes ordered by students through an audio-cassette loan scheme which has been in operating since 1977. Students wanting to hear a radio programme on cassette may obtain up to four programmes at a time by sending a request card to the University's headquarters. In 1981 42,000 programme recordings were requested, and the loan scheme increased the average listening rate by 6 per cent to 44 per cent, at an average cost to the University of 28 pence per programme request. It is clear that even when made originally for radio transmission, programmes available on cassette are more helpful for students than when broadcast. On a five-point scale, the mean helpfulness rating for broadcast radio in 1979 and 1980 was 3.42. When the same material was used on cassette, the helpfulness rating was 3.79.

However, there is a big difference, both in production style and educational effectiveness, between programmes made originally as radio programmes, and programmes created from the beginning for use specifically in a cassette format. Course designers can make full use of the stop-start and review facility, and the hidden nature of the next part of the tape to be played can also be exploited. Thus students can be talked through diagrams, tables or formulae in a text, can stop the tape and carry out activities, and return to the tape for correct answers or comment. Cassettes combined with text allow the simultaneous use of sound and vision, with freedom for the students to move from one medium to another in their own time, and with the ability to rewind and repeat as necessary. Thus students have full control over their use of the medium.

Cassettes cam be used for a variety of educational purposes for which radio is less suitable or convenient: practice leading to mastery of a technique; commenting on diagrams, charts, tables or text; talking students through a home experiment; backing up or commenting on the television programmers; recordings of conversation, interviews, language use and discussions, which can be replayed several times for the purpose of analysis'; and many other uses has designed an audio-cassette package which demonstrates various ways in which audio-cassettes can be used in a home-learning situation.

Academic staff at the Open University like audio-cassettes because they can easily integrate them with the texts as they design their courses. They can take a recorder home and rough out ideas as they develop the text, whereas with a radio programme, with its continuous and uninterrupted flow, it is impossible to develop such close integration between sound and print. The final cassette tape still benefits from being produced to ensure good sound quality and to avoid mistakes or ambiguity in the script, but academics generally feel that they have much more control over the cassette script than with radio.

The Open University students also like audio-cassettes. In a majority of courses where audio-cassettes have been used, students rank them as the most useful course component after the correspondence texts, and in a few course, they have been ranked even higher than the texts. The features that appeal to students are their convenience, the control they have over them and their informality. Students frequently comment that listening to an audio-cassette is like having a personal tutorial in their own room with the course author, a quality that appears to be lacking in most radio programmes no matter how skilfully they are made.

Lastly, cassette distribution is remarkably cheap in large quantities compared with radio transmission cost, which themselves are not expensive. AC60 cassette can be copied, packaged and sent to a student as part of the course materials for less than fifty pence. Even including copying and clerical cost, it is generally cheaper for the Open University to mail cassettes to students than to pay radio transmission costs for two transmission of each programme, which there are less than 1,000 students on a course. Cassettes, though become increasingly more expensive than radio as student numbers increase beyond 1,000.

The initial choice of media for the Open University was made in 1967. Since then, audio-cassettes have been the University's most successful media innovation. Auto-cassettes are more widely used ad more effective than computer-assisted learning, video-cassettes, telephone teaching, or even television and radio . It is surprising then that few other institutions have exploited this cheap, convenient and effective teaching medium. The Open University's success has been due to course teams not using audio-cassettes as lectures, but instead tightly integrating them with the printed material.

Video-cassettes

The pattern regarding audio-cassettes and radio is repeating itself with video-cassettes ad television to some extent, although there are important differences. As with audio-recorders, a video-cassette player in a school gives more flexibility to the teachers in their use of broadcast meterials. However, there are far fewer video-cassette machines in Britain doubled from 1980 to 1981, This brought the number up to only 25 percent, and few schools has more than one, which meant that they could no play back and record at the same time. Nearly every secondary school had a video recorder in 1981, but the average number per school was only two, not really enough to give the case of access and flexibility required in video recording and playback equipment would do more than anything to increase the effectiveness of schools television. It is significant that the increase in equipment over the last five years has been paralleled by an increase in the overall use of television, particularly in secondary schools, Nevertheless, there is still not enough equipment yet in schools to justify the transfer of schools television to night-time transmission although, technically, it is easier to record television than radio off-air because of the in-built clock on most video-cassette machines.

The inner London Education Authority used to distribute its own programmes, and those of the broadcasting organisations, via a cable system to all the schools in its area. Because of the high cost of renting the lines from the post office it closed down its cable service in 1979, since when it has distribute its programmes on video-cassettes. By 1981 over 75 per cent of the primary schools in the ILEA area had bought video-cassette machines, largely due to a deal worked out between ILEA and a commercial rental company which gave the schools large discount prices. ILEA schools pay a nominal rental for the hire of each cassette loaned from their television service.

Nothing is more volatile at the time of writing than the expansion of home ownership of video-cassette machines. At the end of 1983, nearly 30% of all household in Britain had video-cassette machines in their homes, and sales are roughly doubling each year. Furthermore according to the BBC Audience Research Department figures video-cassette machines are just as likely to be found in lower income as in more wealthy households, the rate of growth of video-cassette access is greater in Britain than in any other country. By 1986 it is expected that half the homes in Britain will have a video-cassette machine.

This rapid growth is due to several reasons. Machines can be rented for a little as 10 per month, and there are many high Street shops and back-street dealers from which video-cassette programmes including feature films, can be hired at little cost. Because many of the broadcast programmes are still of high quality, it is also worth while recording these at home, especially since the range of choice at any one time is limited to four channels in the current absence of a widespread cable TV system.

In 1981 11 per cent of Open University students had access to video-cassette recorders in their homes and another 8 percent had easy access to recorders elsewhere. By the end of 1982, 20 percent of Open University students had access to machines in their home and another 22 percent convenient access elsewhere.

The advent of video-cassette technology has caused

often bitter arguments within the Open University, although now its advantages are generally recognised by the academic staff. The Open University experimented as early as 1974 with a video-cassette replay service to students in its South region. Eventually, the University set up a modest loan scheme on a national basis in 1982. The University's reluctance was due to the fact that any video distribution system becomes an additional cost to broadcasting since although the quality of times has deteriorated, the amount of transmission, and hence its cost, has remained the same. Video distribution costs like those for audio-cassettes-therefore have to be found from the University's academic budget, at the expense of alternative academic programmes, such as new courses or more research, and not from the part earmarked for the BBC.

The loan scheme in 1982 was limited to thirty -seven course with low student numbers and courses without repeat transmission times. The scheme was designed to cope with a limit of 20,000 programme requests in the year. In 1983 the scheme was expended to cover eighty-four course, all with less than 850 students. Students obtain copies of programmes by sending in a request card to the University's headquarters. A small stock of each programme recorded in advance has been made and any demands over that basic stock are net by making extra copies. The cassettes are mailed directly to the students homes. Students in 1982 and 1983 could either watch at home or on machines placed in local study centres or colleges. Cassettes are returned by students after use, and stored for re-use. In this way. 20,000 cassette copies can be added each year to the stock, thereby increasing the number of student requests that can be met within a relatively stable budget from year to year. The full cost of the scheme, including the rental of over 240 machines in regional study centres, was 150,000 in 1982.

An evaluation of the first year's operation showed that, in general, the scheme had been successful. Programmes with a single transmission and a cassette loan facility had higher viewing rates than comparable courses with two transmission. The availability of programmes on video-cassette made it easier for students to integrate television with the rest of their studies and increased student's perception of the hopefulness of the programmes. There was also a high demand for cassettes from non-students, mainly from tutors for use in group sessions. How ever, few students used the machines located in study centres. The equipment appealed mainly non-students since fifty-seven machines were stolen from study centres in the first year! Rental for study centre machines accounted for over half the cost of the scheme (80,000), so in response be no national provision of replay machines in study centres in 1984. Regions will be left to make their own arrangements from their own budges. It is expected though that demand for loan copies will increase as more students get their own machines.

Indeed, many more students make their own recordings than borrow through the video-cassette loan scheme. Home recording increased viewing on post-foundation courses by 8 percent in 1983.

The Open University faces difficult situation over the next five to ten years, until most students have access to a video-recorder. It takes two years to plan an Open University course, then it runs for about eight years. Courses are now being planned which will be running in

1993. Some course teams are anxious to design video-programmes which will exploit the educational advantages of cassette facilities, such as the ability to stop, carry out an activity, rewind and review, or pause on a still-frame. It is the lack of student access to video-cassettes machine rather than the cost of physical distribution which makes the University cautious about producing programmes which can only be used on a cassette machine. Calculating the cost of physical distribution of video-cassettes is complicated, and at the time of writing hypothetical, but it appears that it will actually be cheaper to mail video-cassettes to students than to pay for two transmissions when there are less than 500 students on a course, provided cassettes are returned and re-issued each year. This allows for costs of cassette copying, clerical staff, post and packing, and a 10 percent loss or replacement annually. Four programme equivalents would be transferred to an E-120 cassette and mailed to students with their course material. Students would return the cassettes at the end of their course. Over an eight-year course life, the distribution cost would be as little as 1 per student per programme equivalent. Consequently, the University has decided the following policy for all new course from 1985:

(1) Programme on courses with less than 300 students will have no transmissions but will be distributed on video-cassette to student's homes.

(2) Programmes on course with between 300 and 1,000 students will have one television transmission and can also be borrowed on video-cassette through the loan scheme.

(3) Programmes on course with more than 1,000 students

will have two transmissions but will not be available through the loan scheme.

(4) individual course teams may deviate from this policy if they can make a special case.

The aim of the policy is to encourage course teams to design programmes from the outset using either a broadcast or a video format but not confusing the two. It is also hoped that this will encourage a number of course teams to experiment with the design of video-cassettes, to build up experience about the best way to use the format. The policy at the same time limits the number of students who will have to use a video-cassette machine to about 6,000, possibly requiring about 3,000 students still without access to machines to get one.

In the long term, it is possible that only programmes on the foundation courses and two or three large second-level course will be broadcast at convenient times. Programmes on courses with more than 300 students are likely to be made in a video format, but broadcast one during the night for automatic off-air recording, with a loan scheme back-up. Up courses with less than 300 students, the cassettes will be mailed directly to students.

Why does the University believe that there is such a difference between broadcast and video formats? The first Open University course to be designed for use on video-cassettes was EM235, 'Developing Mathematical Thinking', presented for the first time in 1982. It was aimed at teachers and the programmes were planned to be viewed in groups at local teacher centres or schools already equipped with video-replay machines. In fact, about half the students watched in groups, with the rest watching at home on their own. The programmes were designed differently from programmes, although they were transmitted for off-air recording. Each twenty-five-minute programme consisted of a series of segments, each lasting from two to seven minutes, observing children carrying out mathematical operations. After each segment is was planned that the tape should be stopped and followed by group discussion of the segment. Suggested questions for discussion were contained both in the programme itself and in the accompanying broadcast notes.

An evaluation of this course showed that students in groups used the programmes differently from students watching individually. Individual students used the reply facility more, while group students found that the discussion after each segment provided sufficient recall. Individual students were less confident about their interpretation of the material than group students and tended to concentrate on details rather than on more general points. Students in the group situation were sometimes anxious about using the equipment, not always being familiar with it, or were more self-conscious about stopping, starting or replaying the segments when other were present.

This course is perhaps unusual, being designed for group work, and great care must be taken in generalising to video programmes designed from individual use. It does, however, demonstrate that there are different design features of video programmes if the potential of the medium is to be exploited, and their structure and format will differ from broadcast programmes, just as audio-cassettes that exploit their medium differ from radio programmes This principle has by no means permeated to all producers. Many programmes made by ILEA since 1979 still look like broadcast programmes with a continuous, uninterrupted format, for does the Open University's own drug therapy course made for general practitioners, really exploit the cassette medium. Cassettes were used mainly because they would not be seen by the general public and consisted of a series of interviews between doctors and patients but wit no explicit instruction to stop or interrupt the tape.

While video cassette programmes require different production formats from broadcasts, the design features of audio-cassettes will not always be appropriate for video production. The production requirements of a video programme are much more demanding technically and in terms of manpower. This means that recording of material, and its editing, is separate from the preparation of the texts to which it relates, and makes it more difficult at the design stage to develop the very close integration between text and programme that is possible with audio-cassettes, although careful advance planning and editing of both programme and text can go some way towards this. Nor can students so easily integrate video programme and text simultaneously, because they cannot watch video sequence is much more difficult than during an audio sequence will tend to lead to concentration on detail rather than on principles or general points. In practice, this means that video sequences will tend to run for longer without interruption, with interrogation of the material taking place between segments, with some replay to assist. Particularly where students are having to share equipment either a machine at a study centre, with other student waiting to use it, or at home, with the television set wanted by the rest of the family it will be more difficult for student to spend a great deal of time working repeatedly through the cassette. This is less of a problem with audio-cassettes. It is clear that is the next few years there will be scope for a great deal of experiment and innovation to identify be suitable video-cassette format for education.

The most important aspect for both audio-and video-cassettes is the control over the medium that they offer the learner compared with broadcasts. It is worth looking more carefully at this comparison since it highlights some of the unique characteristics of television, as well as certain weaknessès of broadcasting as an instructional medium.

In comparing these two tables, it would be an advantage to have an audio-cassette so that you could look at the framework whiie I comment upon! It will be seen though, that it is difficult for a learner to integrate or relate broadcasts to other learning materials because of the need to catch the broadcast at a set time and the impossibility of stopping or interrupting a programme at a specific point. If ideas or thoughts are stimulated during a broadcast, learners run the risk of either losing the thread of the programme or being unable to follow through their own ideas. Some producers at the Open University have argued that one of the values of a broadcast is its ability to teach learners to think 'on the run', and that this is an essential everyday skill. We have found little evidence that broadcasts do this and some may well argue that education is more concerned with teaching students to think carefully rather than quickly.

With either a broadcast programme or a cassette each individual member of the target audience is sent the same material. No matter how specialised the target audience each individual will vary in ability to learn from the programme. Programme makers have to make assumption about the appropriate level nut there will always be a majority of the audience who will not find the pace quite right in terms of their own learning needs. With recorded material is provided that the level of the material is not too wide off the mark it is possible for learners over a range of abilities to repeat the material until they have mastery over it. Furthermore, with a recording, learners can stop to reflect on the material, analyse it or restructure it, as it best suits them.

Salomon has pointed out that television is particularly rich in the quantity and variety of information it conveys. It uses a wide variety of symbol system-sounds, pictures, colour, movement. Television is also highly ambiguous in the way it conveys meaning. This results from the techniques used in production-camera angles and movement, editing procedures, manipulation of structure and from the richness of the information television conveys. Because of its ambiguity, television material lends itself to a wide variety of interpretations from each individual viewer, many different interpretations being equally valid. This means that each viewer will abstract different meanings from the same programme. Television should therefore be valuable for developing creative or open ended thinking because it forces learners to impose their own construction of meaning from the programme material. If such a hypothesis is correct, it makes it all the more important that learners have the opportunity to explore television material more fully than is possible with a single, unbroken transmission.

Broadcasts thus appear to be much weaker instructionally than cassettes in terms of integration with other material, ease of recall, mastery learning, deep thinking and possibly creative thinking. By their very nature, broadcasts tend towards stimulating more superficial levels of response compared with cassettes or books.

I have left the most controversial, and potentially most challenging implications of cassettes until last. Cassettes could free educators from the dominance that broadcaster have exerted over the design and distribution of educational audio-visual materials. Until recently, distribution of educational audio-visual materials. Until recently, distributing video-visual material widely through formats other than broadcasting has been unrealistic because of the high costs of distribution on a alternative formats, such as film open-reel video tape, and because of the lack of playback equipment in schools or homes. On the other hand, the distribution of broadcasts has been largely seen as a free service from the user's point of view. The increasing accessibility of video-cassettes are changing that relatively low costs of distributing video-cassettes, are changing that situation. With broadcasting, the broadcasting organisations set the priorities, select content, determine style and decide production and technical standards for what they broadcast. It practice, they only transmit material that they themselves have originated.

Video-cassettes can change all that. I is now realistic for other agencies universities, colleges. Local authorities, voluntary organisations, even school-s to commission, produce and distribute effective video material for the specialised audiences that broadcasters have been unable to serve adequately in the past. Costs will depend very much on what kind of programme is required and on whether full or margins costs are changed. There is, however a good deal of spare production capacity, particularly in the public education sector, so marginal costing is often realistic. Highly effective, professionally made half-hour educational vide-cassettes can be produced for between 8,000 and 20,000 depending on the nature of the material. Cheap programmes which nevertheless are very effective in certain contexts if carefully designed can cost as little as 2,000 to produce. This should be compared with a full production to of around 35,000 or an average of 7,000 for a programme budget for a BBC/ Open University television programme.

You get what you for, of course, BBC/Open University programmes often include overseas filming, expensive computer graphic or animation, glossy drama productions, or complex and originally designed physical models. However, for many educational purposes, such expensive facilities are just not necessary. It depends on what the teacher wants to do.

The implications of lower productions costs and relatively low-cost non-broadcast distribution are fare-reaching. Because video distribution costs are related to the number of cassettes to be distributed, video programmes of very small minority audiences become a real economic possibility, provided that there is a framework through which they can be marketed. Secondly, educators can make programmes in the style, peace and format which they believe to be important. There are obvious dangers that the full potential of television will not be developed by people who are not professional broadcasters. On the other hand, there are many able and trained production staff outside broadcasting organisations willing to work to a clear educational brief. Also, those who regularly deal with specialist groups are likely to be better judges of their needs than professional broadcasters There will still probably be a shortage of educators with the talen to exploit the advantage of television on cassette, but the technology does open up the market to those who want to try.

Over the next few years, I foresee rapid expansion of an educational video production and distribution industry in parallel to broadcasting. This in itself is unlikely to lead to the end of educational broadcasting. Broadcaster still have two strong advantages: their programmes are available to schools and the general public at no extra direct cost; and they have a wealth of resource. Experience and a powerful reputation behind them. Non broadcast video is likely to serve rater different needs from those of broadcasters. Nevertheless, there will be areas of overlap, and where the broadcaster do not meet the needs of their target groups, they are likely to lose audiences to enterprising video producer. A number of agencies are now gearing themselves up for production and distribution of non-broadcast educational video. ILEA in particular has a large stock of cassette programmes available for hire by other local authorities, a does the recently established Educational Video Index.

It is unlikely that the commercial television companies will move into producing their own non-broadcast educational video material, but he BBC might, through BBC Enterprises. More likely is that educational broadcasting will be moved to night-time transmission for off-air recording, or be abolished completely, to free the air-waves for extended morning television in order to compete with cable and satellite competition. If the broadcasting organisations do start extensively producing non-broadcast material for education, it will raise some interesting legal and financial issues. Will they reflect the true cost of making the programmes, or will they merely charge copying, marketing and distribution costs? The true cost is likely to be too high for schools. On the other hand, if the price of cassettes does not reflect the true cost, would broadcasting organisations be open to the charge of using license-holders' money or profits from advertising to undercut independent, non-broadcast production companies?

Whatever happens, it will be interesting over the next few years to see whether there will be such an expansion of non-broadcast educational video as predicted, and if so, how the broadcasting organisations will respond to the challenge.

Video-discs and interactive video

There are different manufacturers' formats for video-discs and a variety of models within each format but, nevertheless, the principle of video-disc technology is relatively simple to grasp. The more advanced systems using laser technology allow up to 54,000 single still-frames, with full colour, to be stored on one side of a disc. Each frame can be individually identified and accessed almost instantaneously. The rate at which these frames can be played can be varied across a wide range of speeds, from stepping through single frames, through slow motion, up to normal or even fast speeds. Two high-quality independent sound tracks, capable of synchronization with the pictures when played at motion speed are also available.

These features allow a combination of moving and still pictures to be played linked to stereo or two independent sound-tracks. The systems allow for slow-motion, frame-by-frame presentation, fast motion, fast or slow forward or reverse search, or still-frame presentation, with no picture jitter at all on still-frame, each feature under the direct control of the viewer. More significantly, full computer control over the video-disc player is possible, either using an 'in-board' microcomputer linked to the video-disc player through an 'interface', i.e. a processor or computer programme that allows the microcomputer electronic assess to the video-disc player's controls. With the right interface, it is possible to link up low cost domestic video-disc players with low-cost micro-computers, and to combine graphics or keyboard symbols from the computer with sound and pictures from the video-disc, on the same television set, with pictures from both sources either overlaid, or presented in sequence.

Because the laser-based systems use light to read the disc, there is no mechanical contact. Therefore disc life and quality are not likely to be affected by constant use. Picture and sound quality, even on the cheaper players, is better than on video-cassette machines, although as yet commercial video-disc machine cannot record, only play back. The low-cost simpler domestic models retail at around L400, with the more advanced commercial machines costing L1,200.

Video-discs certainly provide more sophisticated and better quality video and audio facilities than video-cassettes, but it would be a mistake to think of video-disc technology is a distinct teaching medium in its own right, with a unique potential for education, and its own unique requirements for design and production.

Because access, control of speed and search facilities are more refined on video-disc machines, they allow learners even greater control over video materials. Furthermore, by linking video-discs to microcomputers, learners can interact with the video-disc and the computer. This means that the computer can provide feedback to learners on what they have learned from the disc and can guide learner through appropriate 'routes', so that the learning experience is more individualised and suited to each learner's needs.

Video-cassettes can also be linked to computers in this way, but less efficiently than video-discs. Video-cassettes do not have individual frames like video-discs, so on all but the highest-cost machines, it is difficult to get completely still pictures. While it is possible to lay electronic pulses as markers along a video-cassette tap, thus enabling each point on the tape to be identified and accessed, this cannot be done so accurately and cleanly as with a video-disc. It also takes time for video-cassettes to wind backwards and forwards to the point to be accessed, whereas video-disc access is virtually instantaneous. Nervertheless, a microcomputer linked to a video-cassette machine can do many of the things that a video-disc can do, if less elegantly.

At the time of writing, every few educational video-disc have been made, so the educational potential of interactive video is till combines two well-established learning media, video and computer-assisted learning, in the hope that it will bring together the advantages and overcome the deficiencies of both.

So far, three rather different ways of using video-discs in education seem to be emerging. The first is to use video-disc to provide a superior form of control and access. Thus a normal television programme can be made available on disc format, with perhaps a second sound-track added. The learner can then use the still-frame, slow motion and fast search facilities as required. A refinement would be the provision of an index at the start of the disc so that the learner can go immediately to the section of most interest. Such discs can be useful for showing model procedures, such as the correct positions or movements for gymnasts or golfers and the correct procedure for stripping down a car engine. Or for showing animals operating in their natural habitat. The BBC has produced a video-disc of this kind on British garden birds, with of programme but it is possible for those who purchase such a disc to add their own computer control relatively easily. In this way, tests, feedback and suitable routing through the dice dependent on test responses, can all be added through the disc dependent on test response, can all be added through a linked computer.

Alternatively, video-disc and computer control can be designed together as the video-disc is being planned. The resulting package can be extremely complex. Both to design and to work through as a student. Student responses via the computer need not be limited to selecting from an array of multiple-choice answers, but can involve feeding in data, or more complex problem solving. Very sophisticated programmes are possible in this form. Fur instance, a video-disc made at the University of Nebraska provided training on instrument reading or flying light aircraft. After a short period of instruction, the learner is given a set of instrument readings, then has to make decisions about operation of the plane's controls in order to bring the plane in to land. Dependent on the action chose, the disc shows the position of the plane in to land. Dependent on the action chose, the disc shows the position of the plane relative to the earth. This is done by the computer processing the student's answer and selecting the appropriate part of the disc for such an action. Learners can in this way be provided with very realistic simulation exercises with the consequences of their decisions becoming painfully clear! The computer programme that accompanies such a disc can either be physically separate, on cassette or on a computer disc, or it could be computer when played. Computer programmes stored on video-discs, though, can be used only on the type of computer for which the programme was designed. The first commercial interactive educational video-disc, on teaching physics, was made at the University of Nebraska and marketed in 1982 by John Wiley.

There is a third way of using video-discs which is just beginning to be explored in an educational context. Video-discs can provide an efficient and substantial database, with information stored in a variety of ways: as computer data, still-colour pictures, moving pictures, or text. Video-discs could therefore be used as a resource base, which the learner searches or used for a particular purpose. For instance, in training historians, or archaeologists, a whole set of materials could be archived on disc-pictures of archaeological sites and artifacts, historical documents. Short dramatised extracts from historical events, archive film and so on. Students could be asked to work through this material, drawing conclusions and testing hypotheses, with students to some extent imposing their own structure on the organization of the data. A teacher could use the video-disc material to show a sequence of pictures as desired to students. The first such 'archival' video-disc commercially marketed featured the satellite photographs of Jupiter and Saturn.

These are merely glimpses of the potential for education of video-discs. But what are their implications for educational broadcasting? Although the cost of making the master for discs from the final edited tape is not expensive given the cost of production, video-cassette production, are likely to be found mainly in production centres concerned with broadcasting. Secondly, to exploit the advantages of video-disc, programme productions costs are likely to be towards the more expensive end of the scale. Broadcasting organisations thus are well placed to exploit video-disc technology, at least technically.

The design requirements of interactive video-discs and their implication for broadcasting organisations, though, are critical. Where programmes are to be designed from the outside to be used in an integrated way with computer control, difficulties are likely to required form learners, the extent to which learners will be free to choose their own paths through the material, what paths are into the disc, the balance between computer and video graphics, and the design of the computer programme, all have major educational television producer. It would be a fundamental mistake to the normal television production is merely a mild extension of the normal television production process, with the computer programming contracted out as an after though almost. This kind of disc requires a team approach, involving teacher, television producer, computer programmer and instructional designer/evaluator, working as equals from conception to final credits. This inevitably slows up the production process, limits the producer's freedom and increases the cost of production. It will be interesting to see whether broadcasters will be willing to enter into this more complex form of video-disc design and, if so, under what conditions; or whether they will prefer to stick to the safer form of video-disc design, where the disc can stand alone without being tied to pre-determined computer control.

How realistic is it to expect video-discs or interactive video to become widespread in education ? Video-discs have only just come on the market and their commercial viability as a consumer product has yet to be proved. There are at the time of writing few commercial discs available for sale in Britain and it is not yet possible to record off-air on to disc. Video-discs becomes widespread. However, a microcomputer can easily be linked of a video-cassette, in this way replicating many of the functions of video-disc for teaching students at summer school. Particularly for industrial training purposes, where very high-cost technology is being used, such as in nuclear power stations, air-traffic control, or oil-fields, the relatively high cost of interactive video-disc production is irrelevent when set against the phenomenally high cost or disastrous consequences of mistakes made in real circumstances.

The use of video-discs in schools i less certain. The cost of a video-disc machine is not out of the question, but given the slow growth of video-cassette machines with far greater amounts of suitable programme material, I do not see schools rushing to get disc have to cover their full production costs. It is difficult to imagine a well-designed interactive video-disc costing less than L25,000 to produce. To retail at L10 a disc, at least 3,000 discs would need to be sold to recoup costs,- and this is high target for the school market given that there are less than 6,000 secondary schools in Britain. It is likely therefore that video-discs will have a more specialised and restricted use than video-cassettes, at least over the next ten years, but where they are used and well designed they could prove to be extremely valuable.

While the combination of video and computer-assisted learning may bring together the advantages of both, it is as well to remember what Bernard Shaw once said to a lady suggesting an experiment in genetic engineering: But what if it has my looks and your brains? After all, there is only one medium more expensive in education than television-and that is computer-assisted learning. Without careful design and choice of appropriate situations for its use, an interactive videodisc could easily turn out to be horribly ugly and expensive baby.

Cable and satellite

Cable and satellite developments are also likely to have some impact on educational broadcasting, although less immediately than video-cassettes or even video-discs. Should anyone be reading this book in 1988, or beyond, they will no doubt obtain some perverse satisfaction in seeing how wrong my predications have turned out to be, but for reasons which I shall explain, I suspect that there will be no significant expansion of cable for educational purposes much before 1990, although no doubt there will be a number of significant experiments. Similarly, the first UK direct broadcast satellite will not be launched until 1986, and while there will be four DBS television channels available from around that time, none will offer educational services.

Cable and satellite could have major implications for education, but given the slowness with which they are likely to develop in the United Kingdom I shall limit myself to a very brief outline of their potential and limitations and the likely consequences for educational broadcasting.

There are four basic characteristics of cable television that are significant for education: the ability to provide a large number of channels-from thirty to a hundred, dependent on the technology-thereby theoretically increasing choice of service; the possibility of local programming; and the ability to filter or select viewers electronically. Satellite television can provide national coverage but, due to international regulations, Britain is limited to only five channels.

A study of the implications of cable developments for the Open University suggested the following potential advantages of cable for education: better transmission times, more time available for educational television; channels dedicated solely to educational use; access to more potential students; more specifically targeted programming; increased interaction and student participation; improved facilities for local programming by local institutions; more choice of educational programming; easier access to television for teachers; more scope for experiment; multiple sound-track or radio channels.

These are all possible, but whether they are likely depends very much on political and financial decisions yet to be finalised. At the time of writing though, it seems most unlikely that these benefits will be realised in Britain, and, in fact, cable developments are more likely to have negative educational effects. For instance, even the most optimistic forecasts predict that less than 50 percent of the United Kingdom population will be on the cable by the end of the century. Given the current unbridled of commercial basis on which cable is to expand, the first and most profitable areas to be cabled up will be the outer suburban areas and commercial centres of large cities.

Rural communities and the poorer inner city areas are less likely to be cable up quickly, yet this is where the educational need and lack of provision is the greatest.

Currently it seems that there will be no statutory obligation for British cable operators to carry educational or community programmes, unlike practically every other major developed country with cable systems. Nor are there plans yet to ensure the establishment of a nationally linked cable network. Current proposals are based on the establishment of independent local systems. This does not guarantee local programming, though. At least one commentator, John Kowkings, of the International Institute of Communications, predicts that London-based communications companies will make up packages of programming which will then be sold to local stations. The lack of a national network is a severe limitation for the Open University, but if there is spare capacity for local programming this would provide opportunities for other educational institutions to negative deals with stations in their own area.

The key question, though, is who will pay for the educational services on cable, and how? some stations, just to earn brown it points, may allow local college to use spare studio capacity and an otherwise unused channel to provide low-cost programming free of charge. More likely, companies such as Rediffusion Ltd will put together an educational packages of programmes, using whatever existing an educational package or programmes, using whatever existing material it can obtain at nil or low cost from current educational providers, such as those university, colleges and local education authorities that have their own production facilities, Some course may be mounted on a pay-per-view basis, or made available only to student who enrol. Enrolled students could the given an electronic code or key which would enable them to access the relevant programmes.

It is difficult, though, to see coherent educational offerings of any quality being offered in these ways. Educational broadcasts and Open University programmes are strongly protected by copyright, and it is unlikely that such material will be released free of charge fro use by cable operators. The real issue is who is going to pay for the costs of creating original educational material for use on cable. It is unlikely that students will be able to pay the sort of charges that would be necessary to recoup 'true' production costs. At the time of writing there is no lobby for education among the political debates on cable, ad the educational and voluntary agencies seem to be too diverse and unco-ordinated to sort out any agreed policy.

One of the major attractions of cable for education frequently claimed by politicians is its potential for two-way communication, allowing the viewer to interact, respond or participate in the viewing event. This is the sort of claim that needs to be taken with a good pinch of salt. There are major financial and technical obstacles that limit the likelihood of cable being a truly two-way communication system for some time. There are two types of cable that can be laid. Co-axial cable is the basis of virtually all current systems but, for practical purpose, co-axial systems tend to be limited to a maximum of thirty to forty channels in one direction. Co-axial cable is not really suitable as a two-way communication system. Fibre-optic cable has much greater capacity and is a realistic proposition for two-way communication. However, it is still a largely untried technology in a fully operational sense and it will probably be more expensive than co-axial cable to lay.

Seçondly, two-way communication will depend crucially on the configuration or design of the cable system. Co-axial cable uses a 'truck and branch' system, i.e. a central 'truck' cable running down a street with 'branches' off to each house. The street cable itself is probably a branch of a more central trunk running through the town. Even with Fibre-optic cable laid in a truck and branch configuration, 'backward' communication from the home could only follow the same route as the downward signal i.e. back to the 'head-end', the local station. It would not be possible to communicate across branches, i.e. with neighbors in the street, or the local college on the other side of town, unless this communication was relayed from the head-end. If all communication have to go through the head-end, this obviously limits the amount of communications that can be handled, even with a hundred channels.

The alternative, only possible with fibre-optic cable, is a configuration similar to that of the public service telephone system. This has been named a 'star' system since each house would be linked directly to a central switchboard, which in turn would also be linked up with other switchboards. This would allow any one point to communicate directly with any of the others, as with the current telephone system but using much wider bandwidths, including even television transmission' outwards' as well as inwards. Fibre-optic cable would be essential for such a system. Also, a national grid or satellite-linked system would also be necessary for cross-connections between different cable systems. Unfortunately, because of the amount of switching gear required, a star system would be much more expensive to introduce.

For these reasons, interaction is most likely to be limited to user typing. i.e. keying-in instructions along the lines of PRESTEL responses, enabling home banking and possibly some computer assisted learning responses, through a local view data system. In other words, it would give little more than is currently available through PRESTEL. Until a national Fibre-optic star system is established, it will still probably be more practical to use the public telephone network for voice interaction or even telewriting.

These technical considerations indicate quite clearly the king of framework required for education from any national policy for cable development: statutory obligation on cable operators to carry at least one educational and community channel; a policy which will encourage cable operators to provide services in areas of greatest commercially attractive areas; cable systems based on fibre-optics technology 'star cable configurations; and a national grid or a satellite-linked system, for cable allowing inter-communication between all cable users.

Unfortunately, at the time of writing , most of these developments are unlikely for some time given the 'free market' policy of the present Conservative government. The use of cable for educational purposed, therefore, is likely to develop very slowly and to be very piecemeal, as indeed will cable be generally. The original reason for setting up cable systems in North America was to provide decent signals for the many areas not covered by adequate off-air transmission, but in Britain most homes can receive high quality, off-air broadcast transmission.

Secondly, there is no guarantee that an increase in channel will lead to an increase in the range or quality of programmes available. Anyone who has switched from channel to channel on cable systems in America cannot fail to have noticed the similarity of programming on each channel. It is significant that the BBC plans to use one of the new satellite channels merely for repeating old BBC programmes. Leaps in technology are not necessarily accompanied by leaps in imagination. The growth of video-cassette machine ownership, the ease of hiring video-cassettes for a small fee from the local corner shop and the opportunity to record high-quality broadcast programmes, are all real threats to the competitiveness of cable television. Most of all, laying the cables, connecting up homes, providing extra programming and linking cable systems together, will be extremely expensive and financially risky. There is likely to be a great deal of caution exercise, therefore, before there is a major expansion of cable services.

For all these reasons, I am very sceptical of cable being of any significant value for education in the 1980s and early 1990s despite its potential. The main danger of cable developments is that, despite their slow growth, they will put yet more pressure on channel controllers in the broadcasting organisations to remove educational programmes from trasmmission. Only the national broadcasting organisations are in a position during the 1980s and 90s to provide a national educational television service. Cable would be a very poor alternative.

Teletext and viewdata

Teletext systems such a CEEFAX and ORACLE which broadcast 'frames' or 'pages' of information that can be called up at any time by the viewer, have at the moment only two real educational advantages: they are useful for up-dating information, such as news headlines and weather forecasts; and the service is free. Their educational limitations though are considerable. The number of pages that can be accessed is limited, in 1983 to around either hundred, and since each teletext page holds far less information than a printed page, the total amount of information that can be accessed is very small indeed. Because of the inherent nature of the technology, teletext information that can be easily condensed and up-dated. There is no possibility of two-way communication, and a viewer can have irritating time delays while waiting for pages called up. Teletext services have been used, however, for transmitting computer programmes to schools, which are received on a standard aerial and dumped into a BBC microcomputer, again offering a free, if limited, distribution service.

Viewdata systems based on the telephone, such as PRESTEL in Britain. ANTIOPE in France and TELIDON in Canada, have a much wider range of features which may prove more useful in education, but not to the extent of having much impact on broadcasting. Viewdata systems also have major educational limitation. In theory, the number of pages that can be accessed is limited only by the size of the computers that store the pages. However, like teletext systems, the technology limits the amount of information that can be displayed per page. Also, because of the cost of crating and accessing viewdata pages, information again tends to be presented in a condensed and simplified form. Viewdata systems structure information is till unsatisfactory: searching through the branching structure for the information one needs is a tedious business-especially if it was never there in the first place. This technology structures knowledge in a way that is unhelpful for learning. Attempts to base systems on keywords may improve access and structuring, but it is hard to see how the system can ever have the flexibility and richness of an educational television programme.

There have been some experiments, particularly in Canada, to crate teaching materials for use on viewdata systems. TV Ontario located Telidon terminals in 120 primary schools throughout the province, and asked teachers to crate their own programmes by sending in specifications to TV Ontario where skilled Telidon advisers crated the frames and stored them on the mainframe computer. Teachers could then call up on the telephone not only their own programmes but alsc all the other programmes so crated. However, despite the superior picture quality compared with Prestel, the quality of the programmes that I saw was poor, being limited to testing recognition skills. There was of course no sound, and very primitive animation. Pupils appeared restless and easily distracted without the sound facility.

It may be too early yet to judge but it seems there are inherent problems with using systems such as teletext or viewdata extensively in education for teaching purposes, although they may have their use as a data-base or for general informational purposes. If they do have their values, they are more likely to complement than compete with educational broadcasts.

Microcomputers and microcomputer developments

It is the microcomputer which is likely to have the greatest long-term impact on educational broadcasting, as on many other aspects of out lives. Microcomputers will enable individual teachers to crate their own audio-visual teaching materials quickly, easily and economically, and will enable the individual learner to interact in a wide variety of ways with such audio-visual materials, which can be tailor-made to the individual's needs. This material is likely to be highly motivating both for the teacher and the learner. To do this, teachers will not need to be highly skilled in using computers, and the learner need not have any programming expertise to study in this way. Furthermore, this is not a Utopian dream: such a situation could be widespread in British education by the early 1990s. The ability to crate one's own audio-visual materials on microcomputers will not eliminate altogether the need for educational broadcasting but it will require educational broadcasting to be used more precisely.

What evidence do I have for such a bold claim? First, it is important to distinguish between two educational roles for microcomputers. The first is to use them to develop knowledge and skills in computers and computing, since these will be essential requirements for children and many adults in the coming years. But the microcomputer has also the potential to be a very powerful teaching aid in its own right.

Currently, this potential has not been realised, because of technical limitations. Designing computer-assisted learning programmes is at the moment extremely time-consuming, requires a good deal of computer and teaching skills. Effective CAL programmes tend to be expensive to produce in terms of the actual use made of them. The learner is generally limited to responses via the keyboard, and the range of responses in this mode is also limiting, Another very real limitation of CAL is the lack of adequate sound, particularly the teacher's voice. This means that CAL programmes have a heavy reliance on textual and simple graphical presentation, although animation is also available at a price. Crating good quality, effective graphics and animation requires a lot of programming time and can be difficult to achieve on the lower-priced microcomputers. The major limitation, however, at present is the need for teachers to become skilled programmers. Many have neither the time nor the inclination to do this, and in terms of what CAL can currently offer on microcomputers, they are probably correct in assuming that the results are not worth the effort. Those who have proved skillful in this area have tended to produce packages which are used by other teachers-resulting in a degree of centralisation of teaching which in practice limits the use of such materials.

But all that is changing. By the late 1980s peripherals to standard microcomputers, and special packages of programming which can be loaded into a microcomputer so that it can be operated easily in a certain way, will allow teachers to create their own sophisticated audio-visual materials very simply and without needing computer programming skills. Similar developments will also allow audio-visual material to be sent down a telephone line and for learners at home to communicate back with a teacher and other learners, both with voice and visually.

It is possible to predict fairly accurately what a low-cost microcomputer-based audio-visual teaching system will look like partly as a result of experience gained from using a prototype system called CYCLOPS at the open University and in schools. CYCLOPS digitally converts simple animation -into sound codes. These graphics can be very easily generated using a combination of a standard computer keyboard and an electronic writing-pad which also displays graphics on the TV screen. Still images from a video-camera can be similarly coded. Because the video singles are converted into a sound code, they can be stored on audio-cassette or transmitted down standard telephone lines, then decoded back into a video signal. Using either standard stereo audio-cassettes or two telephone lines, full sound can be synchronized with the visuals.

The crucial point is that audio-visual materials can be created very simply and quickly this way without any need for computer programming skills. The system has been successfully used in the Open University for three years for running distance audio-visual telephone tutorials. Students and tutors may be scattered across as many as seven different locations at any one time. Each person though is able to communicate with everyone else taking part, both visually and orally, using a standard teleconference bridge. The same equipment has been used in schools. Three teachers with no previous experience of using computers crated their own CYCLOPS materials for use by individual children in their classes using the audio-cassette facility.

It proved possible in this way to develop very quickly highly motivating and interactive audio-visual materials. CYCLOPS is basically a peripheral system for a standard microcomputer since its core can be made available as cartridge or a ROM to be added to a standard microcomputer.

While it may not be the CYCLOPS system that eventually gets used, by the late 1980s microcomputer-based audio-visual teaching systems will be common in schools. A probable configuration will consist of a standard television receiver, a stereo-cassette player and microphone, a light-pen or an electronic writing-pad, and a standard microcomputer. This will incorparate a CYCLOPS type facility, either built into the microcomputer. itself, or as an add-on accessory, and a connection to the public telephone system. Most of this equipment is already available in schools in British secondary schools were equipped with a microcomputer. The additional components- the light-pen and the CYCLOPS-type carriage- will cost approximately L50 each, and in the future, facilities similar to CYCLOPS are likely to be built into a microcomputer as a standard feature. Microcomputers will also increase in power and reduce in price over the next few years.

With such a facility, teachers can crate their own teaching materials. They can draw on the screen and add text via the keyboard. They can also use standard graphics facilities in the cartridge or the microcomputer itself, to create shapes such as triangles, squares and circles, and to fill-in these shapes with different colours. They can also crate certain forms of animation. The facility ennobles a teacher to build up pictures of frames which are then transferic to a standard audio-cassette. Each picture have been assembled, edited and correctly ordered, the teacher can add the sound-track using the microphone and the audio-cassette player. As well as the teacher's or the pupils voice, music or special effects can be added. The computer controls the length of time each frame is displayed to enable sound-track and picture to be synchronized. The programme can be tested on one or two learners, then amended as necessary. Using the connection with the telephone system, programmes can be exchanged with other schools, ordered from a central bank or used for distance teaching. Teachers can learn how to use the system either by following a simple manual or by loading on a cassette containing a training programme. It is likely to take teachers two or three hours to learn how to use the system, after which time they will have no difficulty in crating their own materials.

Learner will load the audio-cassette and work thought the programme very much in the same way they would work thorough an audio-cassette or video-cassette. In addition, though, they can use the light-pen or keyboard or microphone to give answers to questions on the tape, and their responses can be recorded together with the original programme, for later inspection by the teacher if so desired. CAL features can also be added, with feedback given on keyboard responses, and the tape can be directed to appropriate sections according to the learner's responses.

The technology to do this is already here and will be introduced to schools and colleges in the mid 1980s. We will have to wait and see whether teachers will what to crate their own materials in this way or whether they will prefer to use materials prepared more professionally by others, probably marketed by publishers. Such developments, however, have obvious implications for broadcasters since microcomputer programmes of this kind will have a number of advantages over video materials. They will be much cheaper and easier to produce and distribute than video-cassettes. They will be much more interactive and specific to the needs to individual teachers and learners, especially if created by teachers themselves. But there will also be disadvantages. It is likely that a majority of teachers will prefer high-quality, off-the-shelf material that is readily and easily available. The 'cottage-industry', teacher generated computer materials will still lack many of the features of video, no matter how professional the computer design. There will still be need for film or tape of overseas situations, for portraying human interactions, for presenting the world in a fully representational manner, for the more personal aspects of seeing a human grammes will not eliminate the need for video. They will, however, provide teachers with a convenient and cheaper alternative. Video programmes will therefore have to compete against other highly effective media for the limited time of teachers and learner. If video is to compete successfully, broadcasters and video producers will need to identify and exploit to the full the unique advantages of their medium.

The main developments likely to impact directly on educational broadcasting are cassettes and microcomputers. Both will develop independently of and in parallel with broadcasting, and are likely to reduce to some extent the use of education broadcasts, particularly in schools. Cable and satellite may have a further negative effect, increasing pressure on broadcasting organisations either to transfer educational programmes to inconvenient or impossible times or, for financial reasons, to drop educational programmes altogether. Cable is unlikely though to offer an effective alternative for education. The main overall effect on broadcasters will be the need to identify and exploit the unique educational advantages of broadcasting, since a range of highly effective audio-visual alternatives are now becoming available to teachers and learners.

2

Historical Development of School Broadcast Programmes

School broadcast programme at the international level in developed and developing countries

Radio is one of the powerful mass media used in education. The role of the mass media cannot be overestimated in the developed as well as in the developing countries in the context of information, entertainment and instruction. At one time they cover the distance of thousand miles and reach the houses of millions.

The developed countries are more advanced and well-equipped in respect of mass media than the developing countries and this is due to the poor economic condition and technical known-how on the part of the developing countries. As per the information supplied by Davison, Boylan and Yu,

"Every household in Japan has at least one radio and one TV set and every Japanese has easy access to the broadcasting media, especially to NHK. So when an NHK audience rating says that a programme attracted 43 per cent, it means literally 43 per cent of the whole Japanese population."

Utilization of media in education in the developing countries has rightly been reflected in the views of Faure *et al.*,

> "Mass transmission techniques capable of making educational messages available to millions of children and adults include two of great importance for developing countries: radio and communication satellite relays:

Now the word is being confronted with the explosion of information and knowledge. For their dissemination, advance communication technology is felt essential of the part of both developed and developing countries. In this connection, the words of Mankekar may be quoted here,

> "Today, we are threatened with an overload of information on the one had and an ever-widening communication gap between developed and developing countries on the other, thanks to Western monopoly on the fast-evolving electronic media".

The School Broadcast Programmes operated in different countries are given below:

The British Broadcasting Company was formed in the United Kingdom in the year 1922. Formal educational broadcasting was started in 1924. Since 1926 separate leaflets were prepared for the broadcast programmes as support materials.

The British Broadcasting Company which was redesignated as the British Broadcasting Corporation received its first Chapter in 1927 wherein the triple aims of radio were listed, viz., information, education and entertainment. Then a through investigation was conducted into the effectiveness of school broadcasts. The findings of which led the authorities to reorganize the system and as such the Central Council for School Broadcasting was formed in the year 1929. Again this body was reformed in 1947 and appeared in the name of the School Broadcasting Council.

The British Broadcasting Corporation prepares educational programmes for the schools on the request of the School Broadcasting Council. The central organisation has the S.B. Council for the UK with related councils in Scotland, Wales and Northern Ireland. The council on their part formulate the policy of broadcasting. Both the BBC and the Councils work in close collaboration keeping in touch with the School Broadcasting Departments. The Chairman and nine other members of the UK Council are appointed by the BBC and the remaining thirty-five members are nominated by national educational bodies. The Councils work through Programme Committees comprising of head-teachers, teachers and advisers. There are three Programme Committee-I is for the children upto 8-9 age-groups, Programme Committee-II is for 8-9 to 12-13 age-groups and Programme Committee-III is for 12-13 to 18 age-groups.

The Ccmmittees stated above are concerned with the objectives, suitability and nature of the programme series of their clientele. The School Broadcasting Council meets twice a year and the Programme Committees meet thrice a year. The Secretary is the head of the Council. There is a team of education officers recruited from different parts of the country having a depth of knowledge about the requirements and problems of the schools as well as the potentialities of the broadcasting. They visit schools regularly, organise teachers' meeting, discuss with the students and teachers at the utilization end and review the policy defitting for them.

The overall control and supervision of the educational broadcasting rest with the Controller of Educational Broadcasting of the BBC assisted by the Assisted by the Assistant Controller and the Head of the Educational Broadcasting Services. The duration of the broadcast programme is normally from fifteen to twenty minutes adopting different formats. Notes for teachers are there in all the series of broadcasts. For pupils, some materials also are developed.

Twenty BBC local radio stations are in operation in England. Each of them broadcast locally devised programme. There is an Education producer in each radio station who takes care of providing programmes for the schools. He works closely with local educational institutions in respect of getting resources for programme production. The programmes are based on local interests and needs. They are made usually in collaboration with local people and getting advice from the advisory Panels composed of local educationalists.

Australia

It was the year 1929 when the Australian Broadcasting Company took an attempt for the School Broadcasting. The Planning Committees constituted with the representatives of the schools assisted the company in 1931 to find out ways for the establishment of continuing School Broadcast Service. As a result of which the educational broadcasts for secondary schools began.

The Australian Broadcasting Commission was established as a National body in 1932. Along with disseminating information it accepted the responsibility of educational broadcasting and pursued the development of the system. The Federal School Broadcasts Advisory Committee was born in 1936.

Initially, the cost of producing and distributing broadcast booklets to schools were borne by the ABC. In 1939, the State Departments of Education took the responsibility of producing broadcast booklets. By the end of 1945 some states rendered assistance to the schools desirous of purchasing receiving sets. The organisational structure for educational broadcasting became flexible. The Federal School Broadcasts Advisory Committee and different State Advisory Committees, both of them, included senior educational administrators and eminent educationlists. The concerned sub-committees in each state included members having expertise in the content and teaching of various subjects.

Since 1949 liaison officers were appointed indifferent states with a view providing a vital link between the schools and ABC. They has to supply information on educational broadcasting and programmes to schools and to convey the reactions of the schools to the ABC. By 1950, all states took up the responsibility of providing broadcast booklets to the schools. A conference of educational authorities was organised by ABC in the vear 1946 to explore the scope of radio in education. As decided a number of constructive suggestions were accepted for the development of educational radio.

As a service to the community the Australian Broadcasting Commission prepares radio programmes for the schools under School Broadcasts. The programmes are made in consultation with the curriculum planners, educationists and practicing teachers. Programmers are not imposed on schools and also there in no official obligation upon teachers to use them.

Since education in Australia is a state responsibility, in each of the capital cities of the six states the Australian Broadcasting Commission has a section of its Education Department. Each section used to maintain close liaison with state educational authorities. The programmes are provided as to the need of the schools in that state. There is an Education Advisory Committee consisting of member representatives of the main educational bodies of the state. The committee guides and assists each state section in its work and advises the ABC on State educational policy matters along with trends in education philosophy. The Director-General of Education acts as the Chairman. This Committee further nominates Consultative Committees to advice on the matters relating to the need of the programmes in the specific areas of education, production of programmes and assessment of the programmes on completion. The subject-matter to be included is decided in consultation with the teachers and subject experts.

The Federal Education Broadcasts Advisory Committee advises the ABC on the broad educational policy matter. The committee is formed with the Director of Education of the ABC, Chairman of the six State Committees, and a representative of the Australian Department Education. The radio programmes do not substitute the teacher. They are used in conjunction with other resources.

Every school, at the end of each year, receive information about the coming year's programmes which differs from state to state. Most series are accompanied by teachers' note and many by illustrated pupils' activity booklets. Teachers' notes are most important for all teachers as these highlight the educational purposes of programmes alongwith the outlines of their contents. Apart from their original and primary value in relation to the broadcasts, many of these publications have a continuing value.

With a view to achieving an essential cumulative experience by following the whole series in order, some programmes are planned in series. The rest are planned in such a way that gives independence to the teachers in the selection. The teachers can select individual programmes or groups of programmes as per the requirement for their scheme of work if they do not desire to utilize the whole series transmitted regularly throughout the year on a number of topics. Again, the teachers are all-owned to use brief extracts from recorded programmes which serve as stimulus at some crucial stage of a project.

The programmes broadcast for the schools are more 'open-ended' style which give enough scope to the students to draw their own conclusions on the issues raised in the programmes. All the above programmes are not meant for all the children. The broadcasts differ in class-wise. In order to facilitate the utilization of programmers to a greater extent, repeat programmes are broadcast over radio.

United States of America

The use of radio in school education developed very fast in the United States of America in the thirties. The first broad-cast for class-room was then the Music Appreciation Hour prepared and broadcast by National Broadcasting Company. Another most significant early contributions was the 'American School of the Air'. This was service of the Columbia Broadcasting System. There were daily programmes in the subjects like science, music, history, literature and current events.

There were 202 radio stations operating in the educational institutions prior to 1936. Gradually, the number came down during 1970. The reasons of falling down were the apathy of educators towards radio and the fluctuation in the financing by the legislatures and school boards. Further, most programmes used in the class-rooms before the Second World War were produced by the Commercial Broadcasting Organisations instead of educational institutions. The revival of educational radio took place by the development of FM broadcasting the reservation in 1945 by the Federal Communications Commission. This Commission exercised the power to issue licenses to new stations and cancelled the licenses of the existing ones. In order to make the broadcasting fair it also formulated the ethics and guidelines.

The National Association of Educational Broadcasters (NAEB) is an organisation which has many educational stations. Their headquarters are in Washington, D.C. The radio division of this organisation is directly concerned with the problems and applications relating to educational radio. Another national organisation is the Corporation of Public Broadcasting. This gives direct financial and programming assistance to qualified educational stations. There is facility for tape network services, i.e., exchange of tape-recorded educational programmes in the U.S.A. The National Educational Network is one such network functioning in the United States. This is a project of the NAEB which selects and distributes outstanding educational radio series produced by member stations. About other networks, mention may be made of the

Eastern educational Radio network and special two-way networks for professional education which exist in several states.

It is not easy to give account of educational broadcasting in the USA as the larger and more important stations and networks are private commercial enterprises. Again, the educational broadcasting is largely a matter of private management. But quite a good number of educational programmes are transmitted in the United States and Latin America by the colleges and universities even by municipal and state-owned stations. The Public Broadcasting Service has increased the amount of educational broadcast is not only taken as a support to the teachers but also as an aid for eradication of illiteracy and imparting education to the rural folk in the matters of health and hygiene, agriculture and social superstitions.

Canada

The Canadian Broadcasting Corporation is the principal broadcasting organisation in Canada. It has one main AM radio network in each language along with small FM networks and shortwave transmissions. The Canadian Broadcasting Corporation has thirty-eight principal radio stations and 324 low power relay transmitters together with fifty-two privately owned stations.

The Federal and the provincial organisations are jointly responsible for the school broadcasts in Canada. The liaison of the provincial departments of education with the CBC is kept through their apnointed heads of school broadcasting. On an experimental basis school broadcasts were operating in the early part in various places of Canada. Being motivated with its success, the CBC moved to set up a National Advisory Council on school broadcasting with representatives from educational bodies. The Council, when set up, worked out a pattern of broadcasts for all over the country. The CBC has a school broadcasts department under one supervisor of school broadcasts. With the advice of the Advisory Council, the CBC gives a series of national broadcasts during a year. The provincial authorities get the rest of the school broadcast time. Normally the duration of each programme is twenty minutes.

The educational producer is answerable to CBC with regard tot he quality and effectiveness of the programme. Similarly, the educational director is responsible to his provincial department of education in respect of the content of the programmes.

France

The French State Broadcasting Service (FSBS) devotes more than one-half of its radio output to educational and cultural broadcasts. Education through radio is given to the children of primary as well as secondary grades. Apart from this there are refresher courses for teachers and courses for the students of the university level. The committee appointed for radio broadcasts advises the central administrative body on programmes, schedules and when needed it plans future projects and makes proposals. The use of radio for traffic control on the national scale is very much effective during the late summer, practically when children travel home from school vocations.

Japan

School Broadcasting in Japan starting from the radio school programmes, is 44 years old. These programmes cover kindergarten, elementary school, middle school, high school, and special education school children. These programmes are broadcast everyday from 9 A.M. to 4.30 P.M. except Sunday. But on Saturdays the broadcast only once a week for a duration of 25 minutes only.

The elementary school broadcasting programmes can be classified into two categories; a semi-governmental system called Nihom Hoso Kyokai and private broadcasting systems. The NHK has a nation-wide network for educational programmes of both radio and television. There are also several private broadcasting systems which produce programmes for elementary school education.

In regard to the production of education programmes, NHK has various committees like Central Advisory Committee on School Broadcasting, Script Review Committee, Monitors' Committee. The experts and specialists outside of NHK are taken as the members to these committee. These committees look after the planning, production and utilization aspects of the educational radio programmes like relevance of the programmes contents, nature of programmes to be produced, process of production of programmes and the efficacy of teaching through radio, etc. Besides, there are many specialist staff in NHK. The procedures followed and the methods adopted in the organisation of educational programmes by private broadcasting systems are almost the same as that of NHK's.

The NHK has the provision of yearly timetables of educational programmes, teacher's guides and text-books for pupils which are available with minimum charge. Apart from this, NHK provides subsidies to the teachers' organization for study of school broadcasting. It also assists for holding of various seminars and meetings and carries our research and survey on the educational broadcasting programmes by means of its own research institute.

Since its inauguration in 1933, the educational broadcasting in Japan has been playing a supplementary role for class-room teachers. In other words, the educational broadcasting does not work as a substitute of a good teacher at the elementary level but supplements the teachings of a good teacher. However, experts on educational broadcasting recognize another supplementary role that it provides not only better teaching materials for schools but also opportunities for on-the-spot training of teachers. Teachers can learn much for themselves by utilizing educational programmes for their pupils.

Malaysia

The work relating to the production of educational radio programmes in Malaysia is carried out by the staff of School Broadcasting Service. The preparation and production of programmes is a collective responsibility of educationalists and broadcasters. The School Broadcasting Committee consists of educationists like members of Federal Inspectorate, lecturers of universities and colleges and heads of schools. The type of programmes to be produced is decided by them. There are various subjects panels under this committee which examine the radio scripts and quality of the radio programmes broadcast for schools.

The educational programmes are produced and broadcast in four languages, viz. National Languages, English, Chinese and Tamil. Programmes are broadcast on four days a week, i.e., from Monday to Thursday. They are transmitted through three Radio Malaysia Networks, i.e., Blue, Green and Red. The Blue Network is for the National Schools, Green for the National Type schools and Red Network for the National Type schools.

Besides the normal transmission, special programmes are also broadcast for students and the public during the school holidays. These special programmes include quiz for schools and English Language of BBC recordings, etc. These programmes are entertaining as well as educating. All the programmes, except for the BBC English, are locally produced by producers drawn from the Malaysian Education Service and trained locally/overseas.

The Teachers Notes containing summary of programmes and the work to be done by the teachers before they are listened to by the children and the follow-up activities to be conducted are sent to the teachers every term. The Teachers Notes are prepared and complied by the staff of the Schools Broadcasting Service. Seminars are held from time to time on the utilization of radio broadcasts in educational institutions.

Sri Lanka

There is State Broadcasting Corporation named as Sri Lanka Broadcasting Corporation which has a special division called the Education Service Division. This special division handles the programmes relating to educational broadcasting. A joint committee comprising of Ministry of Education and Sri Lanka Broadcasting Corporation officials lay down policy matters and priorities relating to educational broadcasts. Subject Sub-Committees at the Curriculum Development Division of the Ministry of Education assist the producers and script writers in selecting topics and contents of programmes to ensure their relevance to syllabus requirements and grade level.

The programmes produced for schools are based on school syllabi and are accompanied by support materials for the teachers. The programmes are prepared for primary school students. Junior Secondary School students and out-of-school children. The subjects on which the education programmes are made for the primary schools cover Music and Movement in Sinhalese for the Grades 1 to 5 and English language for the grades 3 to 5. Junior Secondary School starts from Grades 6 to 10. The programmes for the Junior Secondary School students are on different school subjects. The duration of the programmes is half an hour. Apart from these there are general programmes for those seeking out-of-school educational opportunities beyond the Senior Secondary level.

Morning transmission of educational programmes covers four hours per day. About 60 programmes are transmitted per week including repeat programmes. Evening transmission is spread over two hours.

Thailand

It was the year 1953 when the Council of Ministers of Thailand approved the recommendation of the committee specifically appointed with the ministry to study the possibilities of combining technical training in radio skills with an educations broadcasting service. The Ministry of Education appointed a very broad committee expressing its conviction that educational radio belongs to all branches of education. On the 1st January, 1954, the new station began to broadcast home service programmes for the school children, teachers and the general public from 6 to 8 P.M. on all the days of a week except Sunday when the timing is from 4 to 8 P.M. After two years the weak signals were replaced by strong signals and the coverage was increased. As such the wide coverage encouraged the Ministry to supply school broadcasts, mainly as a help for poorly equipped schools situated in rural areas.

There is one main radio station in Bangkok with nine regional stations in the provinces. These regional stations broadcast the same educational programmes which are produced in the main station in Bangkok. The educational radio station in Bangkok is under the management of Educational Information Division, Office of the Under Secretary, Ministry of Education. It was decided to begin with the subjects like English which was offered widely as a second language in Thai schools, music and social studies. In 1958, the first series of school broadcasts went on the air to a limited schools. In 1959, the Ministry decided to make the service available to any school in Thailand that could receive and wished to use broadcasts. Along with the radio broadcast on English, Music and Social Studies, two thirty-minute programmes for teachers were added as well as a daily half-hour of education and entertainment to be heard during the children's lunch hour. The programmes were evaluated and accordingly there was a continuous process of revision and improvement. The officials of the educational services consider it a fact of life for school broadcasts.

The school radio programmes are broadcast according to the fixed schedules from 9 'o' clock in the morning to half-past two in the afternoon with the intention of giving facility to the schools to arrange the programmes in order to conform with the class schedules. The broadcasting agencies provide programme schedules, teachers' hand books and other related materials to the user schools much before the programmes are broadcast over radio. These facilitate the schools to integrate the radio programmes in the class schedules.

Policy determination for the educational broadcasting is the concern of whole ministry. There are three very important working committees. These are assigned to three areas of school broadcast viz., Music, Social Studies and English. The members of the committees are chosen mostly from among teachers who are expert in the subject-matter and whose advice and suggestions are taken into account in planning and producing the programmes. The committees take basic decisions regarding the curriculum to be taught, the assignment to be given to the members in writing of scripts and preparation of teaching aids. After the work is done, the materials are placed before the concerned committees for criticism and revision. The producers take them for production after the same are approved by the committee. At the beginning of the academic session, officials from the ministry go out to speak to educational officers and teachers in the area where the programmes are heard. Conferences including regional are held in various parts of the country for the educational officials, supervisors and teachers. Summer course is held for the teachers using the English radio broadcasts. Representatives are sent to assist the teacher-training institutions in imparting the techniques of using radio in the class-room. The officials from the division of educational information and members of programme working committees advise the teachers in the use of programmes in course of their visit during the school year. The school broadcast supervisors and the teachers using the broadcast write the evaluation sheets.

Bangladesh

Educational broadcasting in Bangladesh, as in other

countries, aims at the improvement of school education. There are six independent radio stations in the country.

There is a special cell of education broadcasting in Radio Bangladesh. This cell produces some curriculum-based programmes for school students in collaboration with the teachers and the Ministry of Education. The programmes mostly on science, language, co-curricular subjects, are broadcast daily in the evening for a duration of half an hour except sundays. Non-formal education programmes in the areas of agriculture, rural development, population control, family planning, health and hygiene, religion, etc. are also broadcast regularly from Radio Bangladesh.

Tanzania

In the year 1954, broadcasts to schools were first started in Tanganyika. Due to small transmitter, a few schools could utilize the programmes. Within two years a bigger transmitter was in operation and the consequence was all the schools throughout the country could make use of the broadcast programmes. In 1960-61, there were 360 primary schools listening approximately but today there are over 9,000 schools getting the benefit. After the introduction of the Universal Primary Education in 1974, every year the number of listening schools is being increased.

In the beginning, the broadcast programmes were intended for M.E. Schools. Since 1959-60, afternoon broadcasts were started for secondary children. It is revealed from research that these broadcasts are also popular among primary school dropouts. Gradually, it became necessary to increase the print materials for the use of primary school teachers on their request for assisting in their own advancement.

Prior to July 1977 and that too after independence, School Radio Broadcasts were administered by the Ministry of Information and Broadcasting through the Director of Radio Tanzania. With the formation of a Media Education Unit in the office of the Commissioner for National Education, School of National education; actual production of programmes is done by Educational Broadcasters from the Ministry of National Education. The technical side of production is done by Radio Tanzania in their own studios. Transmission is done by Radio Transzania. The Ministry of National Education prepared and distributes support materials to the schools.

After a meeting was held between the officials from the Ministry of National Education and Radio Tanzania Das Es Salaam, a School Broadcast Committee was formed in the year 1977 with the members from the National Education, Media Education Unit, Directorates of Preliminary and Secondary Education as well as Teacher and Adult Education, Institute of Education and Adult Education and Head of School Broadcasts along with the members from the Radio Tanzania. Sub-Committees were formed for actual planning of the programmes in conjunction with the Primary, Secondary and teacher Education Division of the Ministry of National education. The Sub-Committees meet once every month but the School Broadcasts Committee meets twice a year to approve the plans placed by the Sub-Committees.

The aim of primary school broadcasts is to bring to the required level the knowledge a primary school leaver acquires after seven years of education. It was envisaged that because of dearth of relevant text books and competent teachers required, school radio can do a lot in fulfilling the gap. Therefore, the programmes strictly follow the curriculum. Four programmes are broadcast for two hours having twenty minutes duration in an average per school day and six days per week. In all 576 programmes are broadcast each school year.

With regard to secondary school broadcasts, two programmes are broadcast for an hour in a school day and that too 5 days a week. In all 240 programmes are broadcast each school year. The secondary broadcasts are also syllabus-based programmes. As to the need of the curriculum some BBC transcriptions are also used to overcome the difficulty of lack of producers and good script-writers.

Since the teachers were not aware of organising radio listening classes, seminars on how to conduct radio lessons were organised in five Regions in 1978. Teachers showed interest in seminars and found them very much useful. Some more such seminars were organised in the following years. Script-writers workshops were also organised to prepare the teachers for contributing good educational scripts with a view to improving the broadcast programmes.

School broadcast programmes at the national level

The Indian Broadcast Company opened its first broadcasting station in Bombay in July 23, 1927. Thereafter Calcutta and Madras stations were opened. The Indian Broadcasting Company was redesignated as Indian State Broadcasting Service in 1930. Again in 1936 it was known as the All-India Radio.

Bombay was the first station to start School Broadcast Programme in 1929 which was occasional in nature. The Madras station took in up in April 1930. But the Calcutta station had its regular school broadcasting programme since November, 1937. The duration of the programme was for 30 minutes and that too twice a week. It was the year of 1938 when the authorities of All-India Radio gave more emphasis on Educational Broadcasting.

All India radio is the only broadcasting agency in India having 88 broadcast station located at different states. The Central office is located at Delhi with one Chief Producer for Educational Broadcasts who looks after the educational broadcasting network. Out of 88 broadcast stations there is provision for production of educational programmes in 44 stations. These stations produce the educational programmes and relay them as wall. There are stations of All-India Radio which neither originate nor relay them.

Primary broadcasts are enrichment programmes the duration of which varies from 15-20 minutes. In some states they are relayed for 3 days a week and income 5 to 6 days per week. The secondary school programmes are syllabus-based and are broadcast for a duration of 15-20 minutes on all days of a week for the Classed VI to X. During Summer Vacation the educational programmes cease to operate. But in some states the primary programmes continue and enrichment ones. Programmes for teachers are broadcast from almost all A.I.R. stations. In 1958, Kerala had broadcast programmes in support of Correspondence Course for the teachers teaching Science to the children of Standard V. Apart from the above certain organisation produce programmes which are relayed by the A.I.R. stations. The Central Institute of English and Foreign Languages. Hyderabad prepares radio lessons in English for school children which are broadcast from different stations for a duration of 20 minutes.

The State Institute of Education, Gujarat produces English lessons under the caption "Teach English- learn English" for her school teachers which are syllabus-oriented. The two lessons are broadcast once a week in each case having the duration of 30 minutes.

A Radio Pilot Project—Teaching, Hindi as first language was taken up in the year 1979-80 by the Central Institute of Educational Technology , National Council of Educational research and Training, New Delhi for the children of 483 schools in Standard I, II and III of Jaipur and Ajmer of Rajasthan for a period or four years . The programmes were broadcast by A.I.R. station Jaipur.

The All-India Radio station having the provision Educational Broadcast Unit has normally the technical know-how persons like a Producer a Production Assistant and a Script-writer for the purpose of production of programmes. The producer decides the topics to be covered for different grades and on various subjects of the secondary school in consultation with the Board of Secondary Education and in some cases the State educational authorities . After finalisation they are put up before the members to the Consultative Panels constituted by the All-India Radio for ratification. These Panels sit once or twice a year with the members from the Educational Department, Directorate of School Education Board or Secondary Education State Council of Educational Research and Training/State Institute of Education, Educational Technology Cell, Inspectorate of School Education Headsor Schools Educationists and personnel working in the field. After the Topics are finalised the station takes the responsibility of their production and transmission.

The school at the state sector utilize the broadcast programmes and send the feedback for their improvement as to the need of the children.

School broadcast programmes in Orissa

The Cuttack Radio Station was established in the year 1948 after the formation of the All-India Radio in 1936. Since 24th October,1960 ,It started producing School Broadcast Programmes for the Students of Secondary School outlined for different subjects and for various grade levels.

These programmes cater to the needs of the school children ranging from class-VI to Class -X. The objectives of this programme are to supplement and enrich the class teaching. For presentation of the programmes different formats viz. dramatization featurisation discussion narration question answer quiz interview and debate are adopted depending on the content of the topic.

The broadcast timing of the programme is from 12.30 P.M. to 12.50 P.M. everyday for a duration of 20 minutes. But on Sunday the timing is from 7.40 A.M. to 8.A.M. for the same duration.

After the establishment of two more radio station one at Jaipore and another at Sambalpur the production of School Broadcast Programme was shared among the three. Accordingly Sambalpur station produces programmes for Class-VI and the remaining station in their turn broadcast the same. Since Cuttack is the parent station programmes meant for Classes-VIII, IX and X are produced three and the other two station relay them.

Apart from the School Broadcast Programmes discussed above the three radio station produce and broadcast independently the educational; programmes for the students or primary classes which do not follow any syllabus.

The duration of primary school programmes is 20 minutes from 7.40 P.M. to 8.00 P.M. everyday except Sunday . The programmes for secondary school teachers are broadcast every Saturday between 8.30 A.M. For duration of 15 minutes with a view to keeping the teachers abreast with the changes in the educational methodology and innovation required for their professional competency.

The Planning is done in a systematic way in respect of Secondary School Broadcasts. This is done for the whole year well in advance. The A.I.R, Cuttack station involves the Board of Secondary Education orissa in planing the programmes and as such it invites the topics from the Subject Committees of the Board to be covered for different grades of pupils and on various school subjects. Then the same are place before the Consultative Panel for approval. The Consultative Panel constituted by the A.I.R. Cuttack has the following types of members— Station Directs and Educational Producers of three radio station viz. Cuttack, Sambalpur and Jaipur, Secretary Education Department or his nominee, Director State Council of Educational Research and Training or his nominee, president Board or Secondary Education or his nominee officer in Charge Educational, Technology Local Inspector of School some experienced Heads of Secondary Schools, educationists and personnel of voluntary organisation working in the field. Over and above some are recruited as invites who are involved in the work. This Committee meets once a year. After finalisation of the topics the concerned A.I.R. stations take the responsibility of producing and transmitting them for the receiving schools.

The A.I.R., Cuttack station also brings out support materials in the form of a booklet for the teachers along with the Programme Schedule. The booklet covers the broadcast topics for different grade levels, the objectives of each topic and the content in a nut-shell along with the teaching points. This also bears the departmental circular of the State Government giving emphasis on the utilization addressed to the field officers from time to time together with a model evaluation devised by Radio Station for giving feedback by the receiving schools. Prior to the beginning of the academic session the materials are supplied by the Radio Station to the schools those who register their name earlier.

The role of educational technology cell

The Educational Technology Cell which came into being in Orissa in the year 1974 has a major role to play at the utilization end. This Cell is working for the development and adequate utilization of S.B. Programmes since its inspection. Since there was no organised institution at the state level to work for the adequate utilization of S.B. Programmes, it took up the task seriously and in a regular manner. With a view to approving the consumer schools with the benefit of the utilization of School Broadcasts and to take initiative in the matter, the E.T. Cell has so far organised a number of meetings and conferences of the Heads and teachers of the secondary schools as well as the Training Schools and the field officers responsible for the school education.

The E.T. Cell organised training courses for the in-service teachers for effective and adequate utilization of school broadcasts. It also organised workshops for the teachers for contributing good educational scripts for quality broadcast.

Evaluation and feedback are no less important than production and utilization. For the improvement of programmes and for wide acceptance by the utilizing schools, the E.T. Cell conducts evaluation of the programmes and sends feedback to all concerned.

3

Context of Educational Radio and Television

Definitions

What count as educational radio and television? It is easy to claim that practically all radio and television programmes have educational potential because they consist of messages that are culture-laden, in the broad sense of the term. Listeners and viewers may therefore learn something from every programme. What individuals learn depends upon their personal experience and abilities as well as upon the content and style of the programme.

In this book, educational radio and television includes the broadcasting of programmes that aim to teach directly and indirectly, and the use of these programmes both in formal and non-formal learning. Figuren 1 displays these relationships. Which permit many different combinations of purpose on the part of broadcasters and use on the part of learners.

Figure 1 Teaching Purposes and Learning Situations for Educational Broadcasting.

		Teaching purpose	
		Direct	Indirect
Learning situation	Formal	Direct formal	Indirect formal
(in classrooms, community centres or at home.)	Non-formal	Direct non-formal	Indirect non-formal

The broadcasters, for example, may specifically programmes that are designed to be used by teachers in school to enhance their student's learning in particular subject areas. The programmes are therefore intended for the formal learning situation; there are examples of such programmes may be a direct teaching one, as in Nicaraguan Mathematics and the Mexican telescundaria, or they may have a largely indirect purpose, such as drama programmes designed to stimulate class discussion or to broaden the range of reading interests, as in much school broadcasting in Europe and North America. It is not in fact surprising that the more confident teachers are, the less they will look for direct teaching programmes and the more they will seek general enrichment programmes, with variations, of course, in different subject areas.

Students learning by correspondence and broadcasting, as in the United Kingdom's Open University or the Republic of Korea's Air Correspondence High School, are also in a formal learning situation, although they study at home. The programmes prepared for them to complement correspondence tuition may sometimes have a direct instructional purpose and sometimes an indirect purpose of maintaining interest and increasing enjoyment of the course.

There are also educational programmes for children an adults that are not related to any specific course. These programmes are designed for non-formal learning, but they may be quite directly instructional, as in teaching literacy, or a foreign language or how to improve crop fertility, or they may again serve indirect learning purposes, by stimulating interest in the development of micro-economics or by building up confidence to improve personal standards of literacy through participation in local classes.

Understanding of these variations is not helped by differences in use of terminology. For example, programmes designed for the formal situation are often described in North America as 'instructional broadcasting, while programmes for non-formal use would generally be included in 'educational broadcasting' or even in 'public broadcasting'. In Europe, both kinds are generally described as 'educational, but the latter sometimes as 'educative'.

As far as the broadcasting systems are concerned, the boundary of educational radio and television is most clearly visible in organizational structures. Broadcasting organizations, both public and private, establish departments for educational radio and television. Occasionally ministries of education establish divisions responsible for broadcasting, and so do universities and other educational institutions. Agencies seeking to educate people who have left the formal educational system obtained production facilities and staff to make programmes and transmit them, in the field of health, agriculture, community development, and so on. Often they create a clearly labelled new section for such work.

To an observer of a given country, therefore, most of

the provision for educational radio and television stands out quite vividly. Its boundary is least clear where programmes are being offered to listeners and viewers who are outside formal education. For example. Sesame street, the American series of programmes for children not yet at school, is avowedly educational. Bellamy Up a Gum Tree, a naturalist's series on British television, is used by older children and adults to educate themselves, but in most countries where it is broadcast it is without links to the formal education system. There are many similar examples that could be drawn from around the world.

Thus it would be wrong to restrict discussion in this book to educational broadcasting that had been labelled as such, or to broadcasting that serves the formal education system. The case studies in Part Two go beyond these boundaries, offering several examples of television for non-formal education and of radio.

In general, however, educational broadcasting exhibits four dominant characteristics:

(1) its programmes are arranged in series to assist cumulative learning;

(2) they are explicitly planned in consultation with external educational advisers;

(3) they are commonly accompanied by other kinds of learning materials, such as textbooks and study guides; and

(4) there is some attempt made to evaluate use of the broadcasts by teachers and students.

The term 'broadcasting' covers the transmission of programmes by several types of distribution systems. The commonest of these, particularly in developing countries, consists of transmitters broadcasting from towers to conventional aerials and receivers for radio and television. In some countries, however, educational broadcasters have access to other systems, ranging from satellite and micro-wave systems to closed-circuit cable systems. None of these has been expressly excluded from consideration in this book, but systems that principally use telephone lines or some form of storage such as tapes or records are not normally counted as broadcasting, and therefore are not discussed here.

Growth of educational radio and television systems

This is not the place for a lengthy historical review, although such reviews have been written for radio and television in general in several countries and, to a more limited extent, for educational broadcasting in particular. Suffice to say that educational radio rose to prominence in the years before the Second World War, particularly in North America and Western Europe, and that educational television blossomed in the years after that war, as more and more countries adopted television. Within the United States, for instance, many educational institutions set up their own radio stations, as Frost describes for the years up to 1937. In the same country, over sixty educational television stations were in operation by 1961, according to Powell, built largely out of capital provided by charitable foundations. Schramm, Lyle and de Sola suggest that non-commercial educational television had it's birth in the United States as late as 1954, but that about seven stations a year were added over the next nine year's. Across the Atlantic, Western European countries followed a similar sequence of technical development, except that instead of educational stations springing up as in the

United States, educational programmes took their place in the context of general broadcasting, using the same studios and transmitters.

The success of educational radio and television in North America and Western Europe caught the attention of international agencies such as UNESCO, and of national agencies providing technical assistance to developing countries. Both radio and television appeared to hold substantial promise for countries without sufficient trained teachers and classrooms. The new educational media, as radio and television were often called in the sixties, were introduced in many countries, often with the assistance of a foreign agency. Thus the books written by Schramm and his colleagues, starting with The New Media Memo to Educational Planners, were commissioned in the late sixties when confidence in educational radio and television was high and people in developing countries very much wanted to know about experience elsewhere as they planned their own systems for the first time. The Schramm series offered general descriptions of some twenty projects in as many countries, as well as the analyses of the first volume.

In contrast, this volume is written at a time when doubts have arisen about the best way in which to use educational broadcasting particularly in developing countries. Western models have not been universally successful when transplanted, and the need for exchange of information between developing countries has increased; in particular, the need for information about organization and management has increased.

Table 1: Catalogue of Countries and Territories Known to be using Educational Radio Programmes in the 1970s

Africa : Algeria, Angola, Benin, Botswana, Burudi, Central African Republic, the Comoros, the Congo, Djibouti, Egypt Ethiopia, Gambia, Ghana. Lvory Coast, Keneya, Lesotho, Libri, Madagascar, Malawi, Mali, Mauritania, Mauritius, Morocco, Niger, Nigeria, Reunion, Rwanda, Senegal, Seychjelles. SierraLeone, Somalia, South Africa, Sudan, Swaziland, Togo, Tunisia, Uganda, United Republic of Cameroon., United Republic of Tanzania, Upper Volta, Western Sahara, Zambia, Zaire, Zimbabwe.

America : Antigua, Baharmas, Barbados, Belize, Bermuda, Canada, Cayman.

North : Island, Costa Rica, Cuba, Dominica, Dominican Republic,EI salvador, Greenlad, Grenada, Guadeloupe Guatemala, Jamaica, Martonoqie. Mexico, Nicarqagua, Panama, St Kitts, St Lucia, St Pierre et Miquelon,

America : Argentina, Bolivia, Brazil, Chile, Colombia, Ecuador, Falkaland Islands,

South : French Guyana Guyana paraguay, Peru, Venezuela.

Asia: Afghanistan, Bahrain, Brunei, Burma, China, Cyuprus, Hong Kong, Inida, Indonesia, Islamic Republic of Iran, Israel, Japan Jordan, Republic of Korea, Kuwait, Lebanon, Malaysia, Maldives, Nepal, Palostan, Philippines, Qatar, Singapore, Sri Lanka, Syrian Arab Republic Taiwan, Thailand, Turkey, Socialist Republic of Viet Nam, Yemen.

Europe : Austria, Belgium, Czeohoslovakia, Denmark, Finland, France, German Democratic Republic, Federal Republic of Germany, Gibraltar Greece, Hungary, Iceland, Italy, Malta, Betherlands, Borway, Poland, Romania, Soviet, Union, Spain, Sweden, Switzerland, Unityed Kingdom, Yugoslavia.

Oceania : Australia, Cook Islands, Fiji, Gilbert Island, New Caledonia, New Hebrides (United Kingdom) New Zealand, Niue, Norfolk Island, Pacific Islands, Papua New Guinea Tonga, Western Samoa.

In 1980 after more than fifty years of educational radio and about thirty years of educational television, where does educational broadcasting stand in the countries of the world? Tables 1 summarize the position. Almost every country claims to use either educational radio or educational television or both. In some countries, total provision may amount to no more than an hour or two a week. In others. It may add up to than a hundred hours in the same period, beamed at a variety of audiences. In a few countries, educational radio and television are still at the experimental stage, serving very small selected groups of listeners or viewers, sometimes numbering less than 1,000. But in most countries, are counted in tens or hundreds of thousands, and, in a few in millions. Without doubt, educational radio and television today must be regarded as mass media, instruments of mass education.

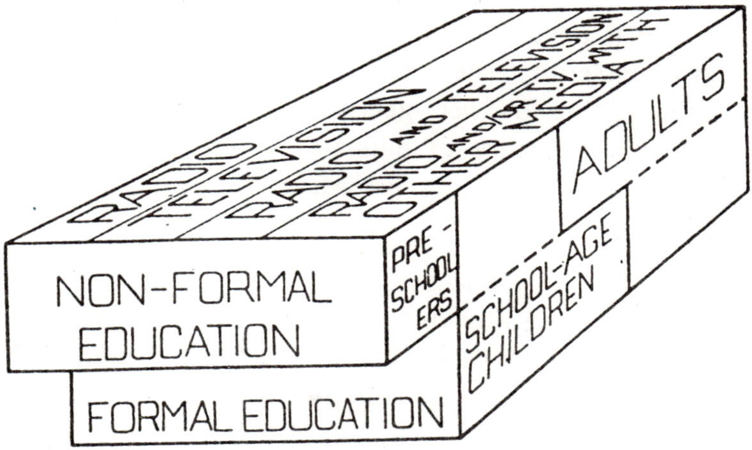

Figure 2. A simple model of the domain of educational radio and television

It would require an extremely compels taxonomy to display the immense variety that exists in educational broadcasting Figure 2 is a simple model of the educational broadcasting domain, analyzed in terms of : (a) field served : (b) media employed : and (c) audiences.

Within each of these three dimensions, a more detailed model could show, for example, the following;

(1) subdivision of the two major fields, in terms of content and purpose of programmes. Formal education is served by programmes, generally in series, in each of the principal subjects learned within the educational system. Non-formal education is served by a much wider range of programmes, from highly structured programmes teaching foreign languages to programmes of general interest, about current affairs, natural history, and so on.

(2) subdivision of the media, in terms of regional or national coverage, types of transmission, means of transmission, the relationship of educational broadcasting to other agencies and to other media, the internal structure of educational broadcasting, its means of finance, its provision for evaluation and feedback, and so on;

(3) subdivision of the audiences, in terms of age, location, time spent on studying, presence of an interpreter, animateur or monitor, size of group, interaction with the broadcasters, participation in activities linked to or dependent upon the broadcasts, scholastic achievement and so on

These are only a few of the categories that could be employed. Only a many-dimensional matrix could contain all, and the number of different combinations that could be derived from them is almost infinite.

There is a real question of who might need such a detailed taxonomy, assuming one could be constructed. Carl Linnaeus, the Swedish naturalist, found his botanical taxonomics invaluable when he wanted to classify and name new plants. But nobody wishes to classify and label educational radio and television systems in such a way. Instead, a detailed taxonomy in this field can do little more than point to systematic variations, without revealing why these variations occur. The reasons for difference lie in the context of each system, therefore it is more valuable to study the context.

Educational radio and television systems in context

Since these systems are largely, if not entirely, the product of local regional and national circumstances, particularly the last, it is hardly surprising that they differ to the extent of no two being identical. It is worth while analyzing the factors that influence planning an implementation. Such factors can be considered under six subheadings: geographical, political, cultural, educational, economic and technical. Figure 3 is a rough map showings the main components that make up each factor. Together they constitute the context of educational radio and television. This grouping is somewhat arbitrary, but provides fairly complete coverage of the factors.

Geographical factors

Terrain and sheer distance are limiting factors for educational broadcasting, as they are for a broadcasting in general. Educational radio for Nepal was planned with that country's mountainous nature very much in mind. Indonesia's Palapa satellite has the potential to beam

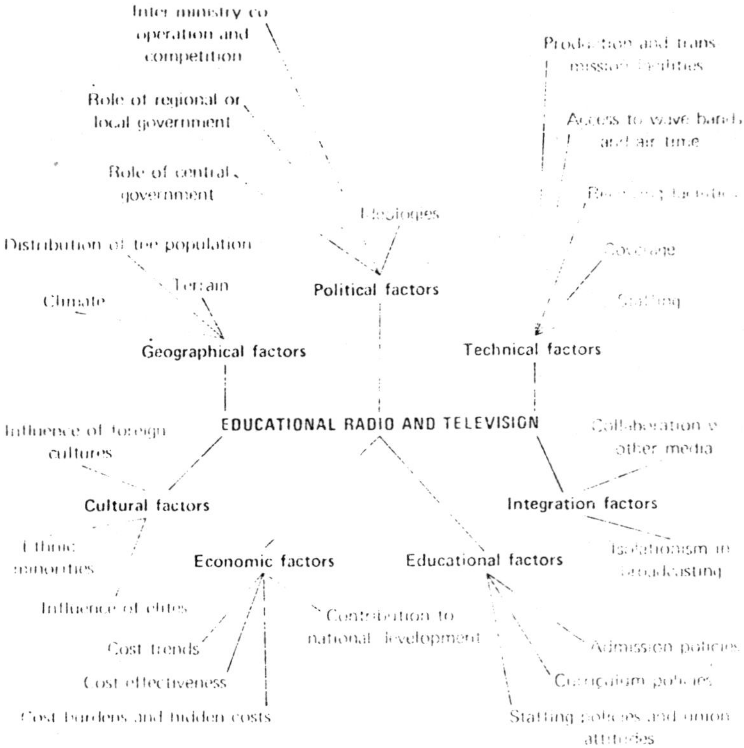

Figure 3. A map of the context of educational radio and television

educational broadcasts to many of the country's 3,000 islands, including ones well beyond the reach of existing ground networks. In the Pacific the satellite code-named ATS-1 has provided for some years an educational link between institutions scattered across that wide ocean. In Canada, more than 80 per cent of the population live close to the southern border, yet remote communities in the tundra are also being served by educational radio and television through a carefully planned combination of distribution systems, including at present the satellite Anik-B.

These are extreme examples, perhaps, and none of them is beyond the experimental state. Yet, even in countries with dense populations and relatively sophisticated communications systems, train and distance must still be taken in to account. In some countries, small but densely populated areas may be in the 'shadow' of a mountain range that deprives students there of educational broadcasts, especially television, as is the case even in parts of the United Kingdom where Open University broadcasts by the British Broadcasting Corporation cannot be received clearly. In a few parts of the United States, in spite of massive investment there in broadcasting systems, some students find themselves too far away from the station that transmits educational programmes. In that country, the public broadcasting network, which carries most of the educational broadcasting network, which carries most of the educational broadcasting, has only recently been linked across the nation by satellite.

It is a fact that many countries build transmitters so that, say, 90 per cent of the population, including all of the urban population, is well served, but the cost of transmitting to far-flung rural areas is too high, and rural populations are frequently placed at a disadvantage. The Maranhao case study in Brazil provides an example of this: in spite of good intentions on the part of planners, only the capital of Maranhao State, Sao Luis, is to date reached by the television transmitter. In Kenya, educational radio transmitters do not reach the rural districts of the north-east, which are sparsely populated. The United Republic of Tanzania, too, has very uneven broadcast coverage. The political incentive to overcome geographical constraints of distance is too small; therefore students in isolated rural districts have to do without educational broadcasts.

Political factors

National ideologies have a powerful influence on broadcasting, particularly educational broadcasting. Broadcasting is easily used as an instrument for raising civic and political awareness or for socialization. Decisions to install radio or television networks rest invariably upon political foundations: even a decision not to install these networks may stem from ideology, as in the case of the United Republic of Tanzania's attitude towards television in the seventies.

A government committed to increasing educational opportunities cannot ignore the potential of educational broadcasting. Likewise, a government wishing to enforce a new national curriculum, possibly against the inclinations of a minority of teachers and students, may use the unifying effect of television of radio. A government fostering decentralization through local or regional development may turn to regional educational broadcasting to help achieve this aim, as in Yugoslavia, or to served ethnic minorities within the country, in Canada. A government seeking to bring about political stability or change by educating the younger generation and re-educating the older will ensure that educational broadcasting contributes to these processes, in harmony with other means.

Government control of broadcasting, particularly educational broadcasting, is strict in many countries, through a variety of agencies. As the case studies show, control may be vested in ministries of education, culture, telecommunications, finance, health, agriculture, industry, internal affair or, occasionally, in an autonomous body on which there is government representation. One or several ministries may be involved in control. Central government in every country retains some measure of control, although in many states local or regional governments exercise control too. Control takes many forms: regulations of all kinds, often administered by a control commission censorship powers membership of boards and advisory committees, financial control through annual funding from a government source, and so on. Educational broadcasting, which usually falls in the public sector rather than the private or commercial, is very vulnerable to struggles for control between ministries: the Ministry of Agriculture may be unwilling to co-operate with the Ministry of Health in producing and transmitting community development programmes, or the Ministry of Telecommunications may neglect to consult other ministries with a legitimate interest in proposed change such as the introduction of satellites. Control of production and transmission facilities is often exercised in an exclusive fashion that deprives possible users of access.

Cultural factors

Ideology also affects government attitudes towards two sets of important cultural factors: the influence of elites and of foreign culture.

In most countries, the influence of elites is so strong that the 'communication effects gap' is probably widening. This gap is between elites and the reminder of the population. Elites employ communications, including educational broadcasting, to their own advantage more than to the advantage of others, with the result that they enhance their own position, claims Rogers. Thus educational broadcasting may be widening the cultural gap, as elites tend to benefit more than others do.

It is difficult to define elites in a universally

acceptable way: their basis may be political, racial, economic or even religious. It is easy to think of modern examples. Education is undoubtedly a way for people to gain entry into elite groups, yet, to the extent that the non-elite class loses its educated members to the elites, that class is weakened in its struggle for social justice.

Such processes of social change, aided and abetted by educational broadcasting, are viewed with varying degrees of favour or disfavour by governments of different ideologies. What is remarkable, as Table 1 shows, is that almost every country of the world, of whatever ideology, has favoured using educational broadcasting to foster social change. Governments seem to ignore the possibility that the communications effect gap may be widening, and consider hat educational broadcasting is in the general interest. Their concern is far more with content.

Educational television, in particular, and to a lesser extent educational radio, may introduce foreign couture. They may introduce new cultural influence that come into sharp conflict the old. The Indian satellite experiment illustrates this conflict vividly: what is the impact of educational television upon people, children and adults, in villages formerly entirely remote from such influence? The Indian government showed great interest in this question, whereas, regrettably, not enough interest in it was displayed by the United States government years ago when educational television was brought to American Samoa for the first time. Similarly, the Ivory Coast Project contain cultural conflict as classroom teacher's authority is challenged by that of the broadcasts, prepared by teachers who are better qualified and , reputedly, more able to teach. In the Ivory Coast, there is also conflict between a national language, French, which is both medium of instruction an vehicled of a foreign culture, and local languages, of which there are many.

The Ivory Coast educational broadcasting project is, of course, a case study of the influence of a metropolitan foreign culture, the culture of a former colonial power, France. Mauritius is another example, where both British and French influences have shaped educational broadcasting. The fact, foreign cultures continue to exert influence on many educational radio and television systems because of the former dominance of certain countries in the field of educational broadcasting. The case studies of the Republican of Korea. Mexico and Nicargua, may not be sufficiently detailed to provide absolute proof of the strong influence of the United States upon educational broadcasting in those countries, yet all contain significant traces of cultural effects, whether in their approach to planning, in their structures, or in their programming. This is hardly surprising when so many of the staff in charge of educational broadcasting systems there have been trained in the United States. Similarly, Canada has been influenced by both the United States and the United Kingdom. In Sweden, the Utbildningsradion otherwise known as the Educational Broadcasting Company has been influenced by European practice, not lest in the United Kingdom, and, to a lesser extent, by North America. All educational broadcasting systems posses uiqueness and their own cultural identity, but within many are clear traces of foreign culture, for better or for worse.

Educational factors

It hardly seems necessary to stress educational factors. Government policies in education have great impact upon educational broadcasting, both television and radio. Consider, for example, national admission policies in the formal education sector. Who should be taught? Most countries in recent years have returned to their sixties goal of achieving universal primary education; secondary and tertiary schooling, after a decade of rapid expansion, now after receive lower priority in the interest of democratization. Yet the demand for education at these higher levels has not slackened. Educational broadcasting may provide a way to supplement existing provision. The El Salvador project was aimed at such supplementation.

Admission policies are not as clearly defined in the non-formal sector, in the sense that participation in, say, a Tanzania radio campaign concerning health does not require formal admission: all are welcome. Nevertheless, decisions about non-formal target audiences are made on educational grounds in part, and influence educational broadcasting for this sector too.

What is to learned? Curriculum policy, itself itself influenced by many cultural factors, also has an impact on educational broadcasting. In most countries, broadcasting organizations and sections of ministries collaborate in attempted to relate programmes to national or regional curricula. Where these curricula are clearly defined, and particularly if they are nationally agreed, it is possible to active fairly close integration. But there are examples of countries with centrally controlled curricula where integration has still proved difficult: Chapter10 on Japan illustrates this. Perhaps the best examples, in this volume, of broadcasting integrated entirely with the classroom curriculum are the Nicareaguan and Ivory Coast projects, yet these are special cases because the classroom curriculum was not the standard one, being specially devised for the projects.

In the non-formal sector the curriculum for educational broadcasting is usually the result of deliberation among interested parties, including the students in some instance. A special curriculum was compiled for the Indian experiment; the research that went into sampling curricula for the Children's Television Workshop is legendary. In both these cases curricula are based on careful consideration of the needs of target audiences. The same could be said about the programming for adults by the BBC in the United Kingdom the adult education broadcasts of UR in Sweden and the work of the Ontario Educational Communications Authority for adults in Canada. All use a variety of methods to determine curricula. The older ones have substantial experience in nonformal education to draw upon too.

Who shall do the teaching? Who shall teach in the classroom and who in the studio? In the classroom, stiffing policies may dictate that less qualified teachers shall depend upon broadcasts to instruct students. This is the pattern in the Mexican telescundaria where relatively poorly trained teachers are asked to monitor or supervise classes at a higher level than they would normally be expected to handle. These classes are taught by television for a part of the day, and the classroom teachers have the tasks of preparing students for the broadcasts and insuring that they complete followed-up activities prescribed by the broadcasters with the backing of the Ministry,. By contrast, classroom teachers are not displaced in the Mexican manner during Nippoh Hoso Kyodai's broadcasting on television and radio for schools. The programmes are intended instead to enrich lessons, and teachers take great interest in learning how to use them for this purpose. On the other hand, teachers are dispensed with altogether in the NHK Gakuen Correspondence High School, excepts as correspondence tuto.ᵴ. Elsewhere, Ivory Coast classroom teachers are temporarily displaced, like those in the Mexican telescundaria, while television teachers take over at a higher standard. In Nicaragua, classroom teachers yield to the radio teachers, again at the higher standard.

Where staffing policies lead to displacement of teachers by broadcasting, sooner or later classroom teachers protest, often through unions that are among the most powerful in the land. In Mexico, the telescundaria classroom teachers sought pay equal to that of their better qualified colleagues who taught at conventional schools of the same level but without television. They did not gain all they sought, party because thy lacked union backing: i the end the government compromised and paid them slightly more than they had been receiving before. Similar problems occurred in EI Salvador as a kind of backlash against the widespread introduction of television into the secondary schools. A proposal to use educational radio to replace teachers in Indonesia was dropped in the face of opposition from teachers and their union,. In fact, strong teacher's unions probably make it impossible for most national governments to employ educational broadcasting to achieve economies through replacing teachers, wholly or in part. Teacher's unions, often a strong influenced in developing countries, may ensure that educational broadcasting is used mainly for enrichment purposes, at least in the formal sector. Where the power of broadcasting has come into conflict with the power of teachers in the classroom, the teachers have won, with few exceptions. In the classroom, the teachers are still doing the teaching.

In the studio too, teachers frequently do the reaching, for both formal and non-formal sectors. That is to say, teachers are employed as presenters, whether by a minister of education, by a college with its own broadcasting station, or by a broadcasting organization. This is not to say that professional presenters, actors, famous people and others are excluded from the studio, nor that educational broadcasting consists largely of teachers talking to camera or microphone. But teachers, usually selected for their ability as expositors, play a major role in creating and presenting educational programmes in many countries. They may also give educational broadcasting greater credibility in the eyes of their classroom colleagues. Their influence cannot be ignored: they are the principal collaborators with professional broadcasters, particularly programme directors, yet the two often conflict, as many of the case studies illustrate.

Who shall judge the effectiveness of educational broadcasting? Usually the judges are not broadcasters but educators, at least for the formal sector. Broadcasters but educators, at least for the formal sector. Broadcasters set their own standards, and judge their own programmes and those of others by these standards, but the ultimate criterion is student achievement. To judge standards, but the ultimate criterion is student achievement. To judge student achievement is difficult and is not usually left to the broadcasters. In some of the case studies, special teams were set up to carry out this evaluation but fundamentally evaluation is a matter for teachers and their supervisors. Results of evaluation can be used powerfully to influence the future of educational programming.

Economic factors

If educational broadcasting contributes to national development through improving education, then this benefit may be set against its costs. But does it do so?

The relationship between education and economic growth was assumed for most of this century to be strong. In the fifties and sixties confident assertions came from economists and educators alike concerning the desirability of more education to fuel economic expansion, not least in developing countries. Moreover, the relationship between lifetime earnings of individuals and their level of education was believed to be strong too. Thus education received economic justification in addition to older and moral justification.

If education fostered economic growth, then surely educational broadcasting, as part of education, could be justified on economic grounds, the more so if it could be shown that broadcasting was a cost effective way of educating large numbers of children and adults, preferably at a lower per capita cost than through face-to-face teaching in classrooms.

Perhaps unfortunately for educational broadcasting, some doubt is now being cast on the strength of the relationship between education and national economic growth. With rate exceptions, developing countries that have devoted large portions of their national budgets to education have not been rewarded by economic expansion. Recent studies of lifetime earning also cast some doubt on the idea of personal investment in education, although in many countries the generalization that better jobs go to better educated people apparently still holds. In some, the over-supply of university graduates and even of secondary school leavers is notoriously large. Finally, doubt is being expressed about whether educational broadcasting can indeed be justified on ground of cost-effectiveness except under certain conditions. It is difficult, as Chapter 6 and 7 demonstrate, to ascertain costs and effected, yet both must be considered by decision -makes in reaching judgments about economic factors related to educational broadcasting planning.

It is worth noting briefly here the distribution of costs of educational broadcasting and who bears the burden of them. Rarely do broadcasters pay, although this is the case in Mexico and a few other countries. In some countries , it is the Ministry of Education that pays broadcasting organizations to produce and transmit programmes. In other, different government agencies provide the subsidy, especially for non-formal programmes. Frequently, however, the full cost does not fall on the 'official provider', because broadcasting organizations or agencies controlling transmission facilities may only charge the marginal cost of providing their services. That is to say, they set their charges at a level lower than that which would be needed to offset all costs, including depreciation of capital equipment, administrative overheads, etc. They spread such basic costs across their main production, and charge additional programmes, such as those for education, at the cost of what they have to pay out to make those programmes. Cost-effectiveness studies prior to 1978 frequently included only marginal costs, thus possibly exaggerating apparent benefits from educational broadcasting. Cost analysis of conventional schooling was not very through either, however, therefore the degree of exaggeration that existed in comparative studies is far from clear.

In general, costs of educational broadcasting have not fallen at all upon the consumer, that is, the student, whether in the formal or nonformal sector. There are a few rare exceptions in formal education: the British Open University, in charging its students fees, could be said to be recovering a small proportion of the money it pays each year to the BBC to make and broadcast its television and radio programmes. The balance of funds needed comes from government subsidy. The Latin American 'radiophonic' schools, operating in the non-formal sector rather than the formal, collect fees too. In Japan, the NHK Gakuen Correspondence High School charges fees. But in all these cases, it would be reasonable to regard the fees as covering the cost of tutoring an perhaps printed material, rather than broadcasting. In no case is the total of educational broadcasting met by students.

Cost are increasingly a constraint upon educational broadcasting. For example, although electronic equipment is becoming cheaper in real terms, technological change can be very costly. The switch to colour in television has implied relatively greater costs, particularly of receivers, compared with black and white. This is a serious problem for developing countries: they cannot continue much longer with monochrome equipment . Manufacture of television transmission equipment is concentrated in a few countries. Most developing countries do not even make their own television receivers. Problems of foreign exchange, particularly the acquisition of hard currency, accompany those of rising costs and the international recession in the face of the oil crisis.

Developed countries seem likely to benefit more, too, from the impact of new high technology on educational broadcasting. In Canada. For example, cable television now provides up to their -six channels to rather more than half the population, thus to some extent relieving educational television of its need to search desperately for suitable air time. In the same country, satellites bring health and other community-oriented programmes to remote villages. Video-recorders, video-discs and teletext, using new forms of electronic storage and transmission, coupled with old forms, posses great potential for educational broadcasting, at least in developed countries. These countries are likely to increase their dominance as producers of equipment and programmes; the North-South dialogue will have to be more effective than to date if developing countries are to participate in and benefit from the communication revolution that seems to be occurring beyond their borders. At present, in the field of educational broadcasting, economic factors create another gap between North and South.

Technical factors

Education broadcasting cannot be effective if it has extremely limited access to wavebands and/or air-time. Access to wavebands is a technical problem: the proliferation of broadcasting stations has led to increasing discussion at international level as interference has become greater. Educational broadcasting, particularly where it serves minority groups and small audiences, has not fared well in the debates. Air-time, particularly during peak hours, has become scarcer, under pressure from professional broadcasters to remove educational programmes to times that are inconvenient for students, leaving peak times free for general broadcasting. There is a crisis in public broadcasting, from which much educational programming emanates, as audiences are lost to commercial stations and costs rise. In the non-formal sector in particular, students who have jobs find they have to listen or view in the early morning or late at night. The problem is less sever for students in classrooms operating during daytime, since these hours are usually considered to be off- peak and are more readily released by broadcasting schedule controllers.

There is no doubt that improved recording equipment can offer technical solutions, at a price, to these problems of access to waveband and air-time. The issue that then arises is more economic than technical: who will pay? If a student has to buy a recorder, or even a player of records, of whatever type, this is an additional cost that may deter him from studying. Yet clearly few organizations can afford to provide such equipment to large number of students, except perhaps at the basic level of a sound tape-player or recorder. As a compromise, they may install equipment in some central place or places and require students to attend to listen or view, thus losing the advantage that broadcasting possesses of reaching into student's homes.

The search for large audiences and for economies of scale induces broadcasters, including those in educational broadcasting, to ask for national, or at least regional , coverage. This too may be a technical matter, involving the linking of stations in networks or perhaps the construction of additional transmitters and repeaters., The extent to which educational broadcasting is able to reach its students may have a strong impact on its perceived effectiveness. If some among a body of students cannot receive broadcasts, others may perceive these broadcasts as more or less necessary, with the consequence that broadcasters themselves feel less inclined to make programmes that can be deemed essential. To some extent, this has happened at the Open University, which, through problems of access and air-time is unable to designate as essential the majority of its broadcasts through the BBC.

Another technical matter is control of the supply, operation and maintenance of production and transmission facilities: studios, control rooms, transmitters and so on. Control may rest with those who have little or nothing to do with educational broadcasting. Educational broadcasters may be wholly dependent upon advice from such technical personnel, who may be influenced more by general broadcasting and national communications policies then by those of educational broadcasting.

To an even greater extent. Control of receiving facilities, including the availability and maintenance of receivers and power supplies lies outside the domain of educational broadcasting. True, there are a few examples to the contrary: the Indian satellite experiment offers a case study of attempts to integrate technical aspects and control with all other factors being considered. Another example of massive foreign support, the Ivory Coast Project, made similar attempts, More usually, however, control rests in the hands of private manufacturers and individual consumers, who must be persuaded rather than coerced.

Choice of transmission systems has significant implications for educational broadcasting Among the case studies in this volume are example of several different systems: the direct broadcast satellite system as recently used for one year in India the ill-fated attempt to use tethered balloons to carry high-altitude television transmitters in the Republic of Korea, the more conventional networks in Mexico or Sweden an the cable system of Canada and the United States.

Each system has its advantages and disadvantages from the point of view of educational broadcasting. Direct broadcast satellites can provide immense geographical coverage: Anik-B in Canada spans the whole country, east and west as well as north south. They can also provide additional channels at relatively low cost compared with terrestrial networks in sparsely populated countries. On the other hand, every receiver requires an aerial that is more expensive than the conventional, or it must be linked to a cable system that has a community aerial feeding signals from the satellite. The extra cost of the special aerial is small when spread across a number of students, or course, but to bring them together when they are widely scattered is to defeat the purpose of direct broadcast satellites, which is to broadcast direct to homes.

Cable television and radio certainly offer to educational broadcasting additional channels and air-time, but they also offer high-quality reproduction, as in say, the fine arts. On the other hand , few countries have cable systems that extend beyond a limited number of densely populated urban areas: the cable companies usually wish to offset the cost of laying comparatively short lengths of cable against revenue from a relatively high number of subscribers. Rural areas are at a disadvantage, even where cable systems are more fully developed, as in North America.

Finally, there is the matter of technical staff, who are in short supply everywhere. Appropriate facilities for training are inadequate. Countries receiving foreign aid to install up-to date educational broadcasting studios and transmitters find themselves without key technical staff to operate the new systems, which are promptly labeled white elephants by politicians- if the teachers have not said it first. Only a few countries offer training schemes. Nationals of developing countries returning home after intensive course using the relatively lavish facilities of, say, France, Japan, the United Kingdom or the United States, do not easily settle down to being operators of small systems without proper technical support, in countries where they were trained , or in the non-educational sector of broadcasting in their own country. Thus the supply and training of technical staff is often a very real constraint in organizing and managing educational radio and television.

Integration with other media.

So far, this chapter has dealt with educational broadcasting per se, without much mention of integration of broadcasting with other media for educational purpose. Nevertheless, it is vital that planners should take a holistic view if they wish educational broadcasting to have maximum impact. Educational broadcasters can easily become isolationists: they may make and transmit the programmes and ignore what happens at the other media simultaneously, to enrich and reinforce the message of broadcasts. Educational broadcasting has been caricatured often enough as a process of one -way communication.

Against this tendency towards isolationism, it must be said that in recent years a good deal had been in may countries to ensure that educational broadcasts on both radio and television are integrated into the fabric of education, whether formal or non-formal. For example, most educational broadcasting is now accompanied by printed material of two or three kinds. There are textbooks or work-books for students in classrooms, and guides and schedules for teachers. The intention at least is that teachers will prepare students to listen or view, that students will respond actively during the broadcast and that teachers and students will follow up the broadcast in appropriate ways, if necessary using a variety of media beyond the printed word. In non-formal education, posters, broadsheets, pamphlets, books, records, cassettes, newspapers and magazines may be provided to assist discussion of the broadcasts, which may be radio farm forums and health campaigns of blockbusting documentary series on television. Sometimes the listeners or viewers gather in group to receive the broadcasts, and conduct their discussions with the printed material to hand, as in the United Republic of Tanzania recently.

One of the foremost examples of integration of media exists in the Open University, and its analogues in other countries. At the Open University, educational radio and television programmes are tied to print, which is the dominant medium in the University's teaching system. In addition, where appropriate, these three media are supplemented by home experiment kits, audio -tapes, slides, computer- aided learning and so on.

Integration is not without its problems, however. Where television is the dominant medium in the teaching system it may drain off a disproportionate amount of resources, as in the University of Mid-American the United States, where a few programmes consumed most of the available money, leaving too little to support other activities in the system. Broadcasting organizations in general appear to have difficulties in allocating sufficient resources to print materials for use with education programmes they broadcast, although there are honorable exceptions. Studio directors, whose future is strongly linked to the quality of the programmes they produce, can be excused for not becoming authors and editors of the printed word as well. Administrators in educational broadcasting must surely take the wider view. NHK in Japan and the BBC in the United Kingdom have had some success in integrating print with their broadcasts in the formal sector. The Children's Television Workshop in the United States is turning more and more towards integration: it now uses many media to supplement and complement its television programmes, and markets them through a very wide range of channels. Its products can be found in bookstores, supermarkets, department stores, toy shops, record and music shops and clothing stores, to say nothing of mail order lists. The Nicaraguan Radio Mathematics Project represents a very high degree of integration of just radio and print since student's progress through the work-books is more or less controlled by the radio programmes.

Integration causes problems for teachers and students as well as broadcasters. Programmes that are linked tightly to texts, for example, must be aired at the right time, or else recorded and used when appropriate. Texts that depend on broadcasts are practically useless if for some unforeseen reason students cannot listen or view. The more tigtly integrated the media, the higher the risks of disruption of student's learning. Texts are usually under student's control except perhaps in some developing countries where they remain under teacher's control. Broadcasts are seldom under student control in any way, and are often beyond classroom teacher's control, accept that both students and teachers can turn them off!

In spite of these difficulties, integration of the media seems likely to increase, particularly in developed countries where new forms of storage and transmission of educational information are becoming available at an accelerating rather. There is no doubt that the next decade will see these forms being used for education as well as for entertainment. Text, not necessarily print, will become more closely integrated than even with the sounds and moving images of television, not necessarily broadcast over the air. Integration will occur not only at the point of reception but also in storage, which will be vastly greater in capacity thank at present; therefore, new ways will be found for exploring what it contains.

In the meantime, most countries, especially those of the Third World, are likely to continue using educational radio and television, combined wherever possible with print.

4

Radio and Television as Media of Mass Communication

Man as a social being cannot help communicating with others. He has to change his ideas and experience, feelings and emotions with his near and dear ones. He communicates with others individually as well as in groups through one or more senses-sight , sound, touch, taste or smell. The modern society has been too complex to unction only through direct communication between one individual and another. Most of our important message must reach many people at a time in order to be effective and meaningful. A house-wife expresses her grievance about the price-rise in her home and neighbourhood, but this reaches a mass audience when she gets a letter to the editor published in a newspaper having wider circulation.

A message can be communicated to a mass audience by many media. The ancient media are the printed materials with words and picture which communicate the message through the sense of sight only. Radio is one of the mass media which communicates message through sense of sound only. But television and films are mass media which are both visual and auditory in nature. There are no watertight compartments among these three kinds of media. All the media are inter-related both in functions and in personnel. A newspaper can bring out an event flashed in a radio programme and a mews published in a daily may be highlighted by radio. Television can utilize a message transmitted both by the newspaper as well as radio with the same objective of bringing about adequate awareness. Similarly, a newspaper reporter having a good voice can become a radio commentator and a radio artist having suitable photogenic appearance can be a TV artist or a film star.

Mass communication media

In this age of science and technology, importance of mass media cannot be overestimated. It is felt difficult to spend a single day without the use of mass media. Deferent aspects of our -social, political, economic, and even personal, are being influenced by mass media.

Public opinion which is the driving force for turning the wheels of any government is moulded by various communication media. In a democracy no government can afford to function, arbitrarily. The people at the helm of affairs must be restrained by public opinion. If they ail to work up to the hopes and aspirations of the common mass, counter forces begin to operate and threaten them with defeat in the next election. It is therefore rightly said that a democracy gets the kind of government that the majority of its people desire and deserve.

Mass media work as an instrument for forming public opinion and expanding our national economy through advertising and publicity. They create as well as reflect people's tastes, needs and requirements which lead to industrial and commercial enterprises. All this promotes economic environment of the country.

Influence of mass media on social relations is extremely significant. No aspect of our behaviour, relationships and habits escapes the impact of the mass media. Our social conditions, neighbor relations, racial issues, student's tensions, marriage ceremonies, eve-teasing, cheap music, fashions in dress, food and so on, are constantly reported and discussed over mass media. Our curiosity to know and imitate is always apt to be influenced by the mass media, sometimes blindly. For example, a new style of dress worn by a popular star in a film can start a national fad and a cheap music on trivial matters like frivolity of ornaments or frailty for other sex may be played again and again.

Radio and television

Radio and Television are the most powerful media at present. Emery and others have rightly said," Television and radio are the electronic carpets that transport millions of persons each day to far away places. They are the twentieth century creations of the technological revolution that has been transforming much of the world for almost two centuries and their impact on our social, political, and cultural life has been profound." Radio and television, although relatively new media, have already made their impression on world civilization very strikingly.

It has been aptly mentioned that short-wave radio has linked the nations for years and now television is bouncing its signal of space satellites and using oceanic cables to transmit live telecasts to and from peoples the world over. Scarcely a country even in Asia and Africa, fails to receive and transmit television programmes. Despite the head start which the United States got in telecasting in the late 1940s families in this country today own fewer than half the sets in the world. The impending cultural, economic and political impact of a worldwide exchange or programmes, including virtually instantaneous coverage of important events in many countries, will be profound.

Radio and television can present the world in no time. These mass media have made dissemination of news, of information, of comment, of entertainment possible on a scale unprecedented in human history. A distinguished media expert, Narayana Menon has nicely observed, "The spoken word was rehabilitated with its full force- or nearly full force and just as the supremacy of sound was being accepted as the key actor in communication., Television overtakes it, the visual element asserting itself again. All this in ones lie time."

Development of radio

On of the pioneering attempts to transmit music and speech over a transmitter was made in 1915 by an American Company. Arlington, to a United States naval station to the Eiffel Tower in Paris, nearly 4,000 miles away. In England the Marconi Station in Chelmsford started broadcasting two daily programmes each of 30 minutes duration. In 1922, a Marconi Station was up in London to form the nucleus of the BBC. In the same year the British Broadcasting Company was formed and its first service was Launched on November 14, 1922. With Mr. J.C.W.Reith as General Manager. This became very popular within two year and broadcasting rapidly became part of the life and the environment of the people. Its control and management became the matters of national concern and interest. On January, 1 1927 the British Broadcasting Corporation came into being and its role was to act "as trustee or the national interest." Parliament was to have the right of ultimate control and Governors of the BBC were to have the maximum freedom possible. Mr Reith, later Sir Reith and subsequently Lord Reith was its first Director General with wide executive powers and worked as the key person with great vision ,initiative and imagination.

In the meantime, America witnessed a number of experiments in broadcasting. Although a section of people opposed the idea of commercial broadcasting and pleaded for making it a public service, advertising was found to be quite attractive in the medium. The commercial possibilities of broadcasting were profitably be explored by industrialists businessmen, churches and others. As many as five hundred station sprang up in the USA by 1924 and commercial broadcasting attracted the maximum audience. A large number of broadcasting networks were set up on private enterprise and problems of control as regards wave-lengths, licensing and so on were confronted by the nation. Consequently, the Congress passed the Radio Act in 1927 and the Federal Radio Commission later redesignated as Federal communication commission was established to function as the controlling body having the power to issue licenses to new stations, to close down existing areas, to set down the ethics and guidelines or air broadcasting. On the whole American broadcasting is mostly private and more independent.

Radio came to India to India late, but not so late. A early as 1924 witnessed radio broadcasting in our country. Soon a Radio Club was formed in Madras and started a broadcasting service. In 1926 got the licences. The first station was stabilised in Bombay on July 23,1927. And the second one in Calcutta on August 26,1927. However, due to the then prevailing political conditions, expenses of the Company were more than the revenues as a result of which the Government grated a licence to the Indian Broadcasting Company was liquidated in 1930. But there was public protests and the Government took over the service which was reorganised into the AIR in 1936.

The AIR, however, had a pathetic and chequered early career. It had to face a lot of administrative problems on account of foreign rule, multiplicity of languages and economic backwardness. As Menon has remarked, "It was only after Independence that broadcasting was organised as a national service. In the last twenty years the growth has been, both in quantity and quality, steady, if not spectacular. The reorientation in outlook, the shift in the emphasis of values, the transformation of an existing set-up into a national service, these take time. And the wheels of Government grind slowly."

In 1947 there were only 14 radio stations out of which 9 were controlled by the AIR, and 5 were managed by the Princely States. But after Independence, 3 stations came under Pakistan and 6 stations were retained by the AIR. So we had only half a dozen stations and about a quarter of a million radio sets throughout India. As such radio reached only about 10 per cent of the population. In 1976 there were 47 stations and another 24 auxiliary stations making a total of 71 transmitting stations. But there were 146 transmitters and 16 million radio sets besides a large number of unlicensed ones. The News Service of the AIR is well-developed and broadcasts news in all the major Indian languages and several dialects. In addition to this there are External Service, tribal programmes, music programmes and so on catering to the needs of various audiences. In 1948 the Cuttack AIR station came into being followed by Sambalpur and Jeypur.

Television

In 1924 John Eaird succeeded in transmitting for the first time a visual across a few feet. Marconi of Italy also tried his hand and for a decade or so experimental television continued. On November 2, 1936, the BBC initiated the first regular television service. There were only 300 television sets at that time and even in England it was not a viable proposition. Suddenly on September, 1, 1939, the BBC television closed down and did not reopen till June 7, 1947. During sixties, however, TV service spread like a wildfire, and its utility caught attention of the world.

In 1956, the General Conference of UNESCO held in New Delhi proposed that a pilot project should be implemented in India to study the use of TV as a medium of education, rural uplift and community development. At last in 1956 an agreement was signed between AIR and UNESCO for stating the project as an experiment in order to assess "the value of different types of Educational Television Programmes suitable for group viewing in rural and urban communities in such a way that the results of such an assessment may be useful not only for Indian but also other Asian countries in the use of television for community education.

During 1960-61 a series of social education programmes were telecast for viewing in various parts of Delhi and the nature as well as degree of the impact of these programmes was evaluated by the National

Fundamental Education centre and Indian Adult Education Association, New Delhi. The results of the experiment were found to be quite encouraging and significantly gainful.

Another project was initiated in the field of school broadcasting in 1961 by the AIR in collaboration with the Ford Foundation. In all 250 schools in Delhi were covered under this project. The TV programmes were directly related to school curriculum and teachers were specially trained for properly utilising them. As the number of schools equipped with TV sets increased, benefits of TV were extended to 36,000 students of science and 96,000 students of English. After four years the impact of the TV programmes was studied by Dr Paul Neurath Government grated a licence to the Indian Broadcasting Company a Professor of Sociology at City University of New York. The overall results of the study was also quite satisfactory. On August 15, 1965 regular TV service was stated in Delhi when Smt. Indira Gandhi was the Minister for Information and Broadcasting. In early 1966, a landmark was made with launching of the Krishi Darshan Programmes for farmers. The AIR was organising this project in collaboroation with the Institute of Agriculture Research, the Delhi Administration and the Atomic Energy Commission. The experiences of this project were enlightening and interesting.

Another epoch-making project was the SITE implemented during the year 1975-76. But the initiative was taken by the UNESCO and nearly a decade back since 1965- the year of international Cooperation. In December, 1965 discussion was made on Space Communication in a meeting of the UNESCO and the experts were asked to advise on this important issue- the use of Space

Communication as a medium for the free flow of information, the spread of education and wider international cultural exchange." An Advisory Panel on Space Communication was set up by UNESCO as decided in the said meeting. An international committee of media experts in a report submitted earlier to the UNESCO after carefully studying the various problems, mentioned, : India as one example, would seem to offer a good choice for the application of a pilot project. The needs of education and development are largely recognised within the country and the present broadcasting facilities are only beginning to play their part.:

It was felt that development of adequate communication facilities by conventional terrestrial means would be comparatively expensive as well as slow. Moreover, India had to tackle a large number of problems like population explosion, food scarcity, mass illiteracy and ignorance. Therefore, the Advisory Panel on Space Communication held in the UNESCO House on March 23,1967 recommended that a pilot study was to be conducted in India. Lastly, the Wildings Groups prepared a favourable feasibility report, communication experts like Wilbur Schram made favourable suggestion and Indian scientists with vision and zeal like Vikram Sarabhai made preliminary arrangements to give the final shape to the project.

The SITE was inaugurated on August 1, 1975 by Smt. Indira Gandhi, the Prime Minister of India at Ahmedabad. The TV programme produced by the AIR, and ISRO were telecast to all the 2,400 selected villages on 21 blocks of 5 states-Andhra Pradesh, Bihar, Karnataka, Madhya Pradesh, Orissa and through the Sateillte loaned by the National Aeronautics and Space

Administration of USA for a period for one year. The Satellite was known as ATS-6 which according to Wernher Von Braun , the distinguished Space scientist "could turn to be the most important advance since movable type as a means of reaching people separated by vast geographical, economic and cultural barriers.

In Orissa 354 center in three revenue districts of Dhenkanal, Phulbani and Sambalpur were selected for the SITE and most of them were located in schools where educational programmes viewed in days time and adult instructional programmes were viewed in the evening hours. During this one year besides formal regular educational programmes some training courses were organised for TV user teachers and science teachers with the use of TV programmes. The studies conducted by the ISRO Ministry of Education, NCERT, Educational Technology Cells and some universities revealed that the impact of SITE on development and Education was quite inspiring.

After the SITE the Government of India decided to provide TV viewing in 40 percent of the villages by setting up low powers terrestrial transmitters in six SITE cluster areas in view of the infrastructure and studio facilities already existing in SITE Continuity programmes. Besides other five SITE States, in Orissa Sambalpur area was selected for the purpose. The program was inaugurated on April 30,1978 and now 15 kms radius of the Sambalpur town. The scheme is popularly known as Community Viewing Scheme and would be of permanent nature with expansion of area and extension of facilities to more schools from time to time.

Radio and TV Complementary

Radio and television are not contradictory to each other may be competitive. In the advance countries where TV had gone a long way and is immensely popular there also media of communication. Both the media are rather cooperative and complementary to each other. In 1960 Western Europe had about 82 million radio stations but by 1970 it had doubled to cover 164 million. Within this decade in japan the number of radio sets had been more than four time and in USA 156 million leaped to 21 millions. An interesting fact in this context may be mentioned here. In USA although there are about 215 million people, the number of radio sets is 320 million. It is quite surprising of course! This may be partly explained by the fact that there are about 10 millions sets fitted in private cars, texis, buses lorries as the Americans spend a good deal of their time in automobiles. In the developing countries television has not yet made any impact and radio had mostly monopolised the broadcasting field.

Every medium had its own strengths and weaknesses. Radio is good in one and bad in the other as TV is satisfying in broadcasting one kind of programmes and may be unsatisfying in another. Radio transmission can cover a vast area with natural barriers and one can listen to radio programmes very well while he is engaged in any physical even in intellectual work. The infrastructure required for radio transmission is also not so sophisticated and expensive like that for TV transmission. Television of course has its own unique and original contributions to make in broadcasting particularly in respect to motions, skills, Artistic desterity. On the whole both media at] potential for mass communication and should be utilised as mutually supporting and supplementing agencies. Both should aim at the universal well-being and education, unprejudiced information and entertainment.

In Orissa radio and TV should develop hand in hand. Radio has already been accepted as an effective medium of communication and TV is yet to take its place in the field. Therefore now there are three Radio Stations and one or two are in the horizon of the State. The Community Viewing Scheme through Terrestrial Transmission is limited to very small area in Sambalpur and its expansion during these last three years is not quite satisfactory. However in view of the INSAT to be available in early 1982 it is hoped that TV transmission would be more popular and wideispread.

5

Formal Education: Strategic Roles for Broadcasting

Justifying educational broadcasting: myth and reality

One should have no illlusions about why educational television or radio systems have sometime been set up. Such decision are rarely taken for any one single reason, but in a number of cases, educational justification have been clearly subordinate to other pressures. Afghanistan is a case in point, if rather an exotic one.

Shortly before the first of the left-wing revolution in 1978, the Afghan government, led by President Daoud, had decided to introduce television for the first time. A studio facility was to be built in the capital, Kabul, with a transmitter to cover Kabul and the surrounding areas initially, and an extension planned later to other parts of the country. The new service was to be opened, President himself, In march 198. The decision to introduce television to Afghanistan was made after a visit from a Japanese technical team and an offer from the Japanese government to provide a low interest loan for the purchase and installation of the basic production and transmission system in Kabul. The main justification for the introduction of television to Afghanistan, which has one of the lowest per-capital income figures for developing countries, was given in the first paragraph of the Japanese International Co-operation Agency's report, proposing in 1975 a television system to the government of Afghanistan: 'Television broadcasting is the most effective media to elevate the level of education to people'.

The transparency of the educational justification became apparent with subsequent events. The facilities covered by the Japanese loan were in fact very limited; the construction of a studio building, the equipment needed for production within that building, the construction of a transmitter covering Kabul and the surrounding area, and a short training programme for Afghan production staff in Japan. It was quite clear to Western experts that substantial amount of additional equipment would be needed to expand production and transmission beyond the very limited levels covered by the loan agreement. This equipment though would have to be bought at full commercial rates.

The government controlled national broadcasting organisation. Radio Kabul, was responsible for the planning and introduction of the television service, assisted by Japanese technical consultants. However, according to Radio Kabul's management, the facilities provided under the Japanese loan agreement were insufficient to allow for the production of any schools programmes or any programmes made specifically for government development agencies,. The facilities would be fully occupied providing news and general programming. Therefore the Ministry of education was instructed to provide a separate educational television service. In order to do this, he ministry of Education had to find additional studio and technical facilities of the production of education programmes, and train its own production staff., since all the training places under the Japanese loan agreement had been allocated to radio Kabul producers for the main service. The Ministry of Education also had to find resources for television receivers in schools, since the Japanese loan agreement covered the provision of only 100 receivers. Most of which were required by Radio Kabul for technical reasons.

The Japanese refuse to extend the loan agreement to include the provision of and educational television production facility or receivers from school use. The ministry of Education therefore tried to raise money from international aid agencies, such as the World Bank, the United Nations Development Programme, or from foreign government agencies, such as USAID, since there was no money earmarked by the Ministry of Finance for the development of an educational television service.

There was little enthusiasm though from the various international and foreign aid agencies from such a project because of the high costs and doubts about the likely effectiveness of such service. Educational television would cover only a limited area around Kabul, which already had better educational provision than the rest of the country. The great majority of the target groups to which the aid agencies were giving priority-the very poor, farmers, children out of school live outside the proposed television transmission area.

Nevertheless, the government was still aiming to provide some form of educational television service for the opening day, In March 1978 even if it meant borrowing films fro other countries. As it happened, these and all the other plan of President Daoud and his government came to an abrupt end in the bloody revolution of 1978. The final irony was that when the Russians arrived six months later, they promptly put to use the brand new, fully operational studio complex and transmitter to explain to the people why they were there. Subsequently, they have scrapped the Japanese system and installed their own.

The example illustrates that while education and development may be the manifest reasons for establishing a television service, in even the poorest countries in the world commercial and political reasons are more likely to be paramount. Daoud was well aware of would enable him to communicate directly with the people. For the Japanese, the loan agreement was clearly a worthwhile commercial proposition, since, for comparatively little cost, hitherto virgin territory would be opened upon for their equipment manufacturers.

Education or development purposes in fact are rarely the main reason for introducing a television service, even in developing countries, Katz and Wedell after a detailed study of eleven developing countries, conclude:

> There is no reason to assume hat the introduction of television is automatically equated with development by the leaders of new and developing nations. Typically, it is introduced for variety of other purposes: as an opiate of the people, as a symbol of nationhood, as a projector of the image of the leadership, as part of a national celebration, to transmit a sporting event, as result of an attractive proposition by a foreign broadcasting company

> or set manufacturer, or to meet the cosmopolitan expectation of big-city dweller demanding to be entertained in the cosmopolitan manner.

However, whatever the original reasons for setting up a television or radio service, it is not difficult to find valid justifications for using it for educational or development purposes, once it is there. There are three broad political objectives in the use of broadcasting in education. The first justifies the use of television and radio by arguing that it can improve the quality foe existing educational provision. The focus in this approach is on the use of television and radio for improvement within he formal education at school or college. This will be the focus of this chapter and the next.

The second political perspective justifies the use of television and radio by arguing that it can equalise or spread more widely educational opportunities- what McAnany and Mayo have called the democratization of educational opportunity. The focus here is on providing educational opportunities beyond the formal school and college system, through part time off campus education for those outside the normal age range or geographical reach of the basic school and college system.

The third is to some extent outside the scope of this book except that it draws attention to some of the limitations of strictly educational television and radio. This justifies the use of television and radio by arguing that they can be used as a revolutionary force, to bring about radical charges in the social structure and in the mobilisation of the poor and oppressed. The focus here is on wider access to the means of broadcast production and distribution, allowing more extensive community use of media, or the use of media as an organising force for local action. The aim here is to by-pass powerful elites, appealing directly to the people.

School broadcasting

> Ask a hundred people in almost any country what they think is meant by educational broadcasting and ninety of them are likely to reply. Well, it means those programmes made for schools,' This is certainly the popular view of educational radio and television; and it has been the starting are of most educational service.

There has been continuous school broadcasting in several Western European countries for over fifty years. The BBC broadcast the first schools radio programme in 1926, and radio broadcasts to schools began in Sweden shortly afterwards. Even since, the annual output of schools broadcasts in Western European countries has bee substantial.

The broadcasting organisations in Britain provide between them a comprehensive range of programmes for schools, offering in any one year programmes of one sort or another for all the age ranges from five to eighteen, and covering most subject areas found in the curriculum of most British schools.

In Britain, the Inner London Education Authority produces its own television programmes for use in schools distributed on videocassettes. In North America, most educational programmes for schools are broadcast, or distributed by cable, usually on a state basis. Programmes are produced by local state educational broadcasting organisations, such as Kentucky Educational Television and the Nebraska Educational Communications Network, by interstate production consortia, such as the Agency for Instructional Television, or by independent local television stations. Consequently in America there is a much greater diversity of educational production than in Britain.

In most developed countries, it has rarely been the intention within the formal education system to use Broadcasting to replace the teacher, or even to reduce staff-pupil ratios; rather, television and radio are seen as an extra resource on which the schools and colleges can draw if they wish. For this reason, I see school of the existing educational service; certainly, in Britain, it is never replacement or substitute for basic educational services.

This attitude might be considered to be due to the way school broadcasts are financed in Britain. The production and transmission of programmes in provided without direct cost to be schools of programmes is provided without direct cost to the schools and purchase the teacher manuals. However, even in the USA, where schools boards pay directly for production if they opt to join one of the Agency for Instructional Television's production concorita, the programmes are still intended as support to existing basic education services, an additional resource for improving the quality of instruction.

When discussing ways in which television and radio have been used to improve the quality of instruction, it will be helpful to distinguish between two rather different ways of generating programmes material. One is to make programmes which are directly aimed at the pupils the second is to aim programmes at the teachers themselves.

Programmes aimed directly at learners

Programmes aimed directly at pupils a students within he

formal educational system can be considered along a continuum from 'enrichment'., through' learning resource', 'meeting special needs', to 'direct teaching and curriculum reform'.

Enrichment

This is perhaps the most common term used to describe the use of schools broadcasting. However, 'enrichment' is rarely clearly defined. I understand enrichment to mean an addition to or a reinforcement of something that the teacher is already trying to do, but which, in itself, is not essential or crucial tot he teaching task. The aim is to use television or radio to reinforce the content, skilis or attitudes that teachers are already committed to important to their pupils or students. This might be done by increasing or relevant, by providing a wider or more realistic context, and so on. The implication behind such a use is that a topic or subject could still be taught or learned without the programme being seen or heard, but that such a programme might increase the chance of learning being more effective, thorough its motivational role.

Learning objectives in such programmes tend to the deliberately vague or diffuse because of the widely varying classroom contexts in which programmes are likely to be used. In countries like Britain, where there is no national curriculum, broadcasters face special difficulties. Below the age at which children begin to follow syllabuses which are publicly examined, each school is more or less free to determine its own curriculum. In many primary schools, what is taught, and even more so how it is taught is very much the choice of individual teachers. Even for the fourteen-to eighteen-year-old age group preparing for public examinations there is no single national syllabus in any subject, since there are several different examination boards and schools are free to choose which they shall follow. Consequently, it is very difficult for educational broadcasters to be sure that their programmes will fit in with the teaching plans of individual classes. It is for this reason that generally, broadcast producers deliberately avoid teaching 'directly' or 'didactically'. It is certainly true that in the past many programmes went out on a wing and a prayer-with the how that somehow they would fit in with, or provide some extra dimension to, the children's learning. Such a use of broadcasting leaves a great deal to chance.

Today, though, British broadcasting organisations would consider their programme policies to be more sophisticated, and it probably does them a disservice to describe the programmes as merely enrichment. Through their advisory councils, which include practicing teachers, and through their advisory councils, which include practising teachers, and through their education officers, who have regular contacts with the schools, British broadcasting organisations are able to get a pretty good idea of the needs of schools and the shift of opinions and trends. As a consequence, most British schools broadcasts are seen by the broadcasters themselves as being much more specific in their educational purpose than just providing enrichment material-although no doubt many programmes are still used in that way by teachers in the schools.

Even in developing countries, which generally have centralise, nationally determined curricula, television or radio are still most frequently used as a support to the standard curriculum. The programmes supplement and reinforce the existing curriculum, which is normally determined without any consideration of how television or radio might be integrated with the curriculum. The programmes supplement and reinforce the existing curriculum, which is normally determine without any consideration of how television or radio might be integrated with the curriculum. Programme designers therefore have to take the curriculum as given, and design their programmes around that curriculum, although they are often guided or advised by the Ministry's curriculum designers. Thus enrichment is till the most common use for schools radio and television in developing countries also, although the World Bank and United States Agency for International Development (USAID) are increasing pressure on developing countries to use radio in particular for direct teaching. Among countries where radio is used to enrich the national curriculum are Thailand and the Philippines, and television is used in a similar way in Singapore, Mauritius, India and Hong Kong.

Programmes styles for enrichment programmes in developed countries are very often similar to the styles of general broadcasts in the documentary and current affairs field. Programmes tend to be loosely structured, sometimes with a magazine format and tend to make use of many of the characteristics of general broadcasting that motivate and hold attention.

Learning resources

One of the main developments in recent years has been to consider television and radio programmes as a learning resources, in that they offer teachers, pupils and students teaching material which would not be easily accessible to them in other ways. A former BBC producer, Richard Hooper, described such a use of television and radio as providing learners with primary resource material. He has argued that until recently teachers have been a substitute source of knowledge and information, storing, trasforming and communicating knowledge to those who have not so far had the opportunity to experience such knowledge to those who have not so far had the opportunity to experience such knowledge for themselves. Television and radio provide learners with access to knowledge and information in a more direct and concrete form. Examples of primary resource material are newsreel and historical film, film from foreign countries or different parts of one's own country, interviews with national leaders or other people in positions of authority interviews with participants in significant events, and so on. Television and radio can also provide learning resources through the construction of physical models, professionally designed graphics and animation, professional performance of dance, drama and music, and foreign languages spoken in context by native speakers. None of this material would otherwise be available in the normal school or college context.

It can be seen that the actual material in programmes used as learning resources is very similar to material found in programmes used for enrichment purposes. The crucial difference is in the way that teachers ad curriculum designers use such material, although there are implications also for the way programmes are designed and structured.

The important difference is that with using television or radio as a learning resource, material from the programmes is closely integrated by the teacher or curriculum designer with other teaching material. Only those parts of the television or radio programmes that are relevant to the teaching task, and which provide different experiences from other materials available, need be used, Ideally, this would mean that when a syllabus is being planned, the likely availability of suitable television or radio material is taken into account before the teaching programme for the term or year is finalised. Such advanced planning however requires access to television and radio material before teaching begins. With the advent of relatively low-cost video and audio cassette recording and reply equipment, this is now much more feasible. It is also feasible in developing countries where there is centralised curriculum planing. Television and radio could be closely integrated with the curriculum so that television, radio, textbooks, direct teaching by the teacher, and group and socialising activities are all integrated. However this could only be done when the curriculum is revised or reformed and, to date, centralised curricula in developing countries have not been designed with integrated television or radio used as a learning resource, as distinct from use for direct teaching.

Nor, of course, is it common for such advanced planning and integration of television and radio to take place in schools in developed countries. However, there are teachers now who do plan the use of television or radio as a learning resource a few days or a week ahead, either using a cassette recording which is already available, or relying on a forthcoming broadcast whose likely contents are well known, from use in previous years. The distinction here between using television or radio as a learning resource or as enrichment is admittedly rather fine. I believe though that there is an important difference between a teacher planning a specific unit of teaching, within which material from a television programme is deliberately chosen because it complements other resource material that the teacher has chose, and using a television programme which it is hoped will relate to other teaching material, but which neither the teacher, nor probably the children, are sure will be relevant.

There are also implications for the design of programmes, when the purpose from the outset is for the material to be used as primary resource material. A programme made for enrichment tends to have a standard length and a unity which allows the programme to stand alone as a meaningful, comprehensive entity. It tends to have an easily recognisable beginning, middle and end. Form a broadcasting organisations point of view, there is much to be said for the enrichment format, in that it can have a dual function within schools for use either as enrichment, or, if used selectively, as resource material, and at the same time be comprehensible to the substantial number of adults who watch or listen to schools broadcasts out of interest.

Programmes made of use as learning resources, particularly if they are made at the outset for cassette distribution and use, should, however, be structured differently. Since teachers will be selecting segments of material, the segments may vary in length and may not even be linked. If made for distribution on cassette, the length of the cassette will be determined by the number and length of the individual segments. Activities may be built in at the end of each segment or edited in such a way that they can be omitted if the teacher chooses. There may be cues in the middle of segments where teachers can stop the programme to ask questions or to allow children to carry out some work before returning to the tape. Commentary is likely to be even less directive or

Instructional than on enrichment programmes; in some cases there will be no commentary.

The aim behind such material is for it to be integrated by teachers into a wider learning experience, where the learning or teaching of facts or concepts is dealt with not just in the programme material nor primarily by the teachers telling the students or pupils, but as a results of the full experience provided by a variety of learning materials and experiences.

However, it must be emphasized that the use of television or radio material in such a deliberately planned, integrated manner is still extremely rare in schools and colleges.

Meeting special needs

Even in the best education service, temporary deficiencies can occur in a particular school due to the loss through sickness, transfer or retirement of specialist staff. Even in developed countries like Britain and the U.S.A. there can be chronic or permanent shortages of specialist stand, particular for science or mathematics teaching. Schools television and radio programmes, by using the skills of experienced and able specialist teachers, can make those skills available to all the schools in the country. Such programmes can be particularly useful to otherwise trained staff who nevertheless be covering areas in which they feel they lack sufficient academic qualifications. Such teachers will be well able to provide suitable follow-up work, to answer questions and to prepare themselves adequately by means of the teachers handbook which accompany the series, but the programmes themselves provide valuable guidance and confidence in following a certain approach. Similarly, as well as specialist staff, schools may lack specialist equipment, such as musical instruments. Television and radio can be useful substitute in such circumstances.

Schools television and radio programmes thus provide extra flexibility in schools, allowing sometimes scarce learning resources to be made available to all schools. Such a role is particularly useful in areas with low population densities, where it would be uneconomical to provide a school with all the facilities found in large urban schools, in areas such as run-down inner city locations in developed countries, or remote rural areas in developing countries, where it can be particularly difficult to recruit scarce specialist staff.

When television and radio programmes are used to meet such deficiencies, a different style of programming may be required from that most appropriate for use as enrichment or learning resources. Since the teachers whom the programmes are aiming to help are not well qualified in the subject area, the programmes will be more useful if they are more didactic and directive, if teachers notes that provide reinforcement and further explanation of the subject material are also available, and if clear follow -up activities are firmly suggested.

Direct teaching and curriculum reform

Perhaps the most spectacular use of the media of instruction in developing countries has been to try to accomplish a swift reform of a national or territorial system of education. Time is of the essence in this sort of project changes that would ordinarily take fifty to one hundred years. At the usual measured pace of education, are projected to be achieved in ten or twenty years.

Television and radio have been used in several developing countries for direct teaching. Both the core content and the style or method of instruction are embodied in the programmes themselves. When television or radio are used in this way within the formal school system there is still a need for adult supervision-although in some projects unqualified monitors have been used instead of trained teachers-but the role of the teacher or monitor is supplement and support the television or radio teaching. The adult then becomes a classroom supervision, organisor and manager but not someone who determines either the content or the method by which the content will be taught. Thus the programmes are the curriculum.

Direct teaching through television and radio has been used in the formal school systems of developing countries in three related but slightly different ways:

(1) to expand the range of the school system, enabling pupils who would otherwise have had no formal schooling beyond a certain age to continue with their schooling. In such a circumstances the government aims to provide education for all children in the relevant age groups in principle to provide the necessary facilities for all such pupils. In this situation, lesson based on the standard national curriculum are distributed by television or radio to areas where there is no adequate conventional school provision. Pupils normally follow the programmes in classes, using basic accommodation. There is usually a supervisor or monitor in charge of the group. Examples of such projects are the Radioprimaria and Telesecundaria projects in Mexico, and ETV Maranhao in Brazil. In some cases, as with the Radio Schools of Australia

pupils study at home with one of their parents as the supervisor. In this case, there is the possibility of to-way communication, as the pupils can talk back on their own radio to the distant teacher.

(2) to improve the quality of instruction, where there are schools, but due to the low level of education of the teachers or their lack of training, and the lack of other suitable resources, such as books, the quality of instruction is considered to be poor. Once again, programmes based on an already existing national curriculum are transmitter, but in this case to other wise conventional schools. An example of this approach is the Radio Mathematics project in Nicaragua. The methods used in his project are being applied also to mathematics teaching in the Philippines and Thailand;

(3) to reform the national school curriculum, in such a way that both the subject matter and the method of teaching are radically changed, with television playing the central, direct teaching role. Television is in this situation both the medium and the catalyst for reform. To data, and perhaps surprisingly, radio has not yet been used in this way, and when television and curriculum reform have been introduced together, it has always been in the form of direct teaching. Television has been used for curriculum reform in American Samoa, El Salvador, the Ivory Coast and Niger.

Curriculum reform of course is possible without the introduction of television; television could also be systematically introduced as part of curriculum reform without it necessarily playing a direct teaching rôle. For instance, only a part of the curriculum need be built around television, or television could be one of several resources available to teachers within a new curriculum. However, there are strong reasons why the introduction of curriculum reform combined with television has resulted in the use of television for direct teaching. A successful reform of a national curriculum thorough conventional methods requires teachers who are already in service, and used to the old curriculum, to be retrained in the new subject material and new methods of teaching. Conventional retaining methods would require special courses, involve travel costs and personal inconvenience to the teachers and may require the withdrawal of teachers from their normal teaching activities. In many developing countries it is the initial training of teachers which receives priority. In such countries planners may fear that the retraining of teachers required by a national curriculum reform through conventional methods would take too long, would be impractical on a large scale and would be too expensive. What better then than to use television to by-pass the retraining problem completed by using television to carry the main burden of teaching the new curriculum? Also, combining curriculum reform with the opening of a new television service provides a clear target and stimulus for curriculum reform. The day on which the television service opens provides a deadline for the introduction of a new curriculum, a deadline which it would embarrassing politically to miss.

It is necessary to have worked on such projects, or at least to have read detailed accounts of them, to comprehend fully their ambition and the difficulties they have had to overcome. The Ivory Coast system required not only the construction of a TV production centre, the training of the staff to run it and the production of 500 hours programming in one year alone, but also the installation and maintenance of battery-operated television sets in over 5,000 classes, many in isolated, humid villages in the bush. As well as a reform of the curriculum, the Ivory Coast project also involved training teachers in the use of television-based education ad required the distribution of over 200 tons of support print materials schools system in American Samoa, in one year the ETV unit was producing 6,000 programmes. In Nicaragua, the programme designers found it necessary to teach mathematics directly by radio to children in rural and poor urban primary schools without printed support materials for the pupils, as these would have substantially increased project costs. They also managed to continue the project successfully through the major part of a bloody revolution. ETV Maranhao provides secondary education by way of television classes which run semi-autonomously through a system of group activities to pupils from very poor homes in a remote part of the Amazon basin in Brazil. This projects is particularly unusual in that it is virtually independent of foreign financial or technical assistance.

In short, the use of television and radio for direct teaching and curriculum reform in developing countries has required-and obtained-a great deal of commitment, hard work, idealism and ingenuity. It has affected large numbers of pupils, teachers and educational planners, and required assistance from foreign consultants, a good deal of foreign financial aid and substantial financial resources from developing counties themselves.

To understand why television and radio have been used in these ways in developing countries-but hardly ever in developed countries-it is necessary to understand the educational needs which led politicians and planners to adopt such radical measures. In Nigar, before the introduction of the educational television project, only 7 per cent of school-age children actually attended school. In the Ivory Coast, 25 per cent of children in target age range attended school in the first grade, but by the fourth grade this figure had dropped to 14 per cent. This was in 1967-68, just before the inception of the television-based reform. At that time, the government's goal was to provide universal primary education through the first six grades by 1985. In El Salvador government, however, considered that it was essential to increase substantially enrolments at this level if its plans for economic growth were to succeed. At the same time, the national curriculum was recognised by the government to be based on values ad concepts imported from Europe in the nineteenth century or individuals. In American Samoa teachers prior to the introduction of the television system were not generally educated beyond 9th grade and they had little command of English, although this was supposed to be the language of instruction in the schools.

There are certain common characteristics of those countries where direct teaching by television and radio have been used. They are typified by low enrolments in the formal school system; high drop-out by those who do enrol; poorly qualified teachers; lack of adequate buildings, books and other basic educational resources; a rapidly increasing population; an uneven distribution of educational resources, with education being more readily available in urban areas and being taken up more by children from more prosperous families; a need for more skilled and semi-skilled workers; and a low national gross income, resulting in severe shortage of money for educational purposes, Politicians and planners in these countries looked to television and radio as a means to break through these major obstacles to educational economic progress.

There are also certain common characteristics about the projects themselves where direct teaching has been used.

(1) The decision to use television or radio for national curriculum reform was heavily influenced by the availability of funding or technical assistance form abroad;

(2) all the countries had a centralise, national curriculum;

(3) all the counties had a low educational base before the introduction of television or radio for direct teaching;

(4) most of the countries were relatively .small and centralised, so schools could be easily reached by a central TV signal.

The use of the television or radio for direct teaching in schools has been restricted to developing countries; there are hardly any examples of its use this way in developed countries.

6

Asia: The Satellite Instuctional Television Experiment in India

Although the satellite instructional Television Experiment in India was in large part a technical feasibility study of satellite transmission in a developing county, it had an important educational broadcasting component. This chapter is based on a case study of the organization and management of SITE's educational broadcasting written by Kiran Karnik a senior staff member in the Indian space research organisation, which was responsible for overall planning of the project.

Context

Site was based on a 1969 agreement between India's Department of Atomic Energy and the national Aeronautics and Space Administration of the United State. India wanted to stimulate national development and gain experience in satellite broadcasting. The united state wanted to demonstrate the potential value of satellite technology for mass communications in developing countries. India carried out a number of pilot studies, including an agricultural television project in villages near

Delhi, before setting up the experiment. The United state sent into space a powerful satellite, ATS-6, capable for receiving signals from earth transmitters ad broadcasting directly to cheaply produced antennae located in India's remote villages. These 3m antennae, made of chicken wire were part of direct reception systems that fed signals from the satellite to large television sets in the schools for use by children in the mornings and adults in the evenings.

As the satellite was able to broadcast to large part of India, over 2,330 villages were included in the experiment in six geographical clusters. Clustering the villages mad maintenance of equipment easier and provided comparatively homogeneous groups of a sufficiently large size for social research. Studies were undertaken to establish the needs of the villagers who could be served by television and to identify the characteristics of the audiences.

The experiment was limited duration, however, since the satellite was made available only for one year.

Organizational structure

The organization structure of SITE was complex because of the involvement of a number of agencies as well as on account of the project's multiple objective. There was, however, a period of debate before agreement was reached. For example., the Indian Space Research organisation had originally hoped to have no responsibility for producing programmes and it wished to have contract with other agencies for the social evaluation.

Karnik does not go into detail concerning the organizational structure of Doordarshan other wise known as Television-India , which was formed from part of All-India Radio in the middle of the project's life. AIR then

DD, was responsible for programme production center and transmitters for the majority of the television programmes DD ,s structure was centralized, with Delhi controlling other stations. It had the capacity to produce very quickly the extremely large number of programmes needed by SITE.

Karnik doe offer an account if ISRO's organizational structure, however, and this is summarized in Figure 12.2. At the higher level, ministries of the national government of India were represented on the Secretaries Committee, which considered national policy regarding SITE, with participation fro potential user ministries such as Health Educational Agriculture as well as from provider ministries, namely space and information and Broadcasting. For more specific decisions, two interministerial committees were created to co-ordinate SITE, but in fact they were not very active. The Secretaries for space and for information and Broadcasting, responsible respectively for ISRO and AIR/DD, constituted the Apex Committee for the project and this committee took ultimate decision regarding collaboration between the two organisation.

Yet, Say Karnik, the all important ISRO-AIR/DD interaction took place primarily through the ISRO-AIR/DD working Group, which consisted of persons actually responsible for SITE from the two its decision were automatically ratified by the Apex committee. The group turned out to be very effective; it could not afford to reach an impasse although frequently there was lengthy and heated debate. This effectiveness was the more remarkable in view of considerable organization differences between ISRO and AIR/DD. The latter was an operational agency with many years of experiences says karnik, while ISRO was relatively a new research and development group with no previous experience in television programme production or utilization. AIR/DD was a programme production organization, ISRO an engineering group with a technological focus.

The Programme Manager for SITE had overall responsibility for the project within ISRO. Several ISRO division were given specific areas of responsibility heads of these division, which had other work as well as SITE, were designated project managers for the SITE activities in their Divisions. Project Managers were involved in two lines of management: to the Programme Manager, SITE, as well as to the Chairman of ISRO. The Chairman of ISRO is Secretary for space in the government.

Within site was a management office, supporting the work of the programme manager and of the SITE management Board, which was made up of the project managers, the Programme Manager and the Manager of the office. This office organized organizations. If there was no disagreement in the Working Group, to the he scheduling, budgeting, manpower and facility planning and liaison with idea and foreign agency., The Board was the focal point for considerable team work among the Project Managers. The Boards took major decision about ISRO's role in SITE, or sent recommendations to the chairman of ISRO for final decision. In general, there was considerable delegation of authority within he project, leading to decentralization under the co-ordination Meeting involving all ISRO's SITE component; production transmission, earth station operations, direct receiving station maintenance, research and so on.

Certain Divisions of ISRO, such as Electronic System,

developed low-cost television equipment for use during SITE including the direct reception systems which had easily replaceable components to aid maintenance. Within ISRO, a software system group was established to carry out programme production to assist utilization and to carry out social research and evaluation. Three cells of staff were responsible for these three areas of activity. The manager of the production cell was in Ahmedabad; he had an Executive Producer at the other ISRO programme production central in Bombay. The engineers in these two centers, however, reported to the head of the Electronic systems Division, and this caused some difficulty as well as bringing benefit in the form of modified or newly developed studio hardware. The manager of the Production Cell delegated approval at various stages of programmes planning to several other committees, but ISRO television producers had considerable freedom in planning and executing their programmes within ISRO general objectives.

Karnik summarizes the objective for site, laid down in the original India-American agreement, as general, instructional and technical.

General objectives

Gain experience in the development, testing and management of a satellite based INSTRUCTIONAL television system, particularly in rural areas, and to determine optimal system parameters. Demonstrate the potential value of satellite technology in the rapid development of effective mass communications in developing countries. Demonstrate the potential value of satellite television broadcasts in the practical instruction of village inhabitants. Stimulate national development in India, with important managerial, economic, technological and social implications.

Instructional objectives.

Undertaken instruction in the fields of family planning, agriculture, national integration, education, teacher training, etc.

Technical objectives

Provide a system test or satellite television broadcasts for national development. Enhance Indian capability in the design, manufacture, deployment, installation operation and maintenance of broadcast and/ or distribution facilities. Gain an opportunity to determine optimum receiver density, distribution and scheduling;' to determine techniques of audience attraction and organization, and to solve problems involved in developing, preparing, presenting and transmitting television programmes.

These objective were kept under review by SITE"s various committees but were not changed during the project. In addition, a statement of objectives was drawn up for programme production for each major series, such as the science series for children. This formed the basis for detailed briefs for each programme.

Production

personnel

AIR/DD staff for SITE were trains or retrained at India's UNESCO ASSISTED Television Training Center ISRO was obliged to recruit staff with no previous television training or experience, but saw in this an advantage. Such staff were free of preconceptions and had not been trained within urban television, which was modeled on television develop countries; therefore they were able to take a fresh approach to the problems of producing instructional programmes for rural community viewing. In fact, of ISRO's fifteen producers in SITE only one had television experience, but all had been trained in film production, most of them in a three year post graduate course within he Film institute of India. ISRO's cameramen film editors and sound recordists had also been trained at the Film Institute. Production assistants were recruited from local theatre groups.

Together, AIR/DD and ISRO had about 35 producers, 250 other production staff and 140 technical staff working on SITE.

ISRO producers encountered difficulties of various kinds; for example, several had to learn a new language, Gujarati, that was being used for some of the transmission. Other had to earn new subject matter for ISRO's science programmes. They had to work with user ministers, especially the extension agencies even to the extent of training a few of the staff of one co-operative dairy to television producers themselves. Such local personnel had something important to say to rural audiences, and Isro's producer could help them to say it on television, but satellite.

In general;, however, ISRO ad difficulty in finding subject matter experts who not only knew their facts but also knew how to work in a team with producers and other ISRO staff. There was also a scarcity of trained evaluators of television programmes; only two could be found both foreign trained, one for Ahmedabad and one for Bombay.

Management of ISRO's Bombay Production

The Bombay studio was responsible for producing about

150 science education programmes for schools, each of 10-12 minutes' duration. Although this work feel with the production cell, immediate authority I Bombay was vested in a an Executive Producer, who had the help of a production manager. The task of the latter was to facilitate production by making available at appropriate times the scarce facilities and manpower.

Plan for this studio were drawn up based on an estimate of the total production required. These included targets for each month and for each producer. Producers raw up work schedules by the most, based on transmission schedule. Test schedules allows days for each production process; shooting, editing, assembling, recording, etc. A master production schedule was drawn up by the manager of the production Cell so that facilities and resources were used to the best advantage. Once these plans had been laid, producers, had almost complete authority during programme making, although there had to be various informal meetings to insure continued coordination. Flexibility was retained by means of a weekly productions schedule that updated the master schedule, and by means of a call sheet issued jointly by the producer an the Production manager forty eight hours before actual shooting of recording. In spite of these safeguards, however, schedules sometime had to be changed at the last minute; a few low priority programmes that could be made at very shot notice were kept in reserve in order to avoid leaving the facilities idle on these occasions.

To monitor production, the production Manger required a Daily Production Report fro each producer shooting or recording. This report contained details of any problems as well as a routine account of what had been done. Form producers; reports, the manager compile his own Daily Report, then used the Week's daily reports to prepare a Weekly Summary, and in turn, and Monthly Report Providing an overview of SITE management of what ad occurred, analyzing performance in relation to targets Each week the Programme preview committee saw programmes, partly to approve them for transmission partly to evaluate producer's work.

ISRO's decision to use teams caused certain delays: producers were unable to dodo much until programme content had been finalized, then had a great deal to do. The production manager had the task of inorganic out these peaks and valleys in individual productivity, while maintaining a steady overall output.

Operational procedures in ISRO's programme production

A set of broad objectives, confined in the Credo, formed the basis upon which programme briefs were written. Each brief centered on a particular topic and laid down the objective of the programme, its relevance to the rural child, the suggested approach and a take off point. Each proper then close a set of briefs on the same topic; he or she made the programmes for that topic unless than manger of the Production cell was obliged to change the allocation to insure full coverage of topic without duplication.

A team was gathered together to make each programme. Content experts mostly came from one of the institutions with which ISRO had formal agreements. The scriptwriter was sometimes the proper himself. The social researcher on ISRO's Bombay staff was member of every team. Once a script had been producer within the teem, it usually had to be approved by the script committee, which looked at it suitability for the target audience, its relationship to the Credo and its literary value. programmes on agriculture, health and science did not go through the committee but were finalized in consultation with appropriate experts, once the script was agreed, the producer was responsible for working out a detailed plan; for casting for choosing appropriate music in consultation with the music director; for scheduling rehearsals, music recordings transport and so on; for budgeting and operating the budget; for reporting; for pretesting for presenting his programmes to the preview Committee and for preparing note on each programme fro teacher use.

Utilization

The user agencies were substantially involved in selecting program content but not as much in utilization, in spite of India's considerable extension infrastructure. Committees set up to co-ordinate utilization had little effect. ISRO did carry out a limited experiment in the area of agriculture and health, however, involving one block in each SITE cluster of villages, In each block, five villages with television sets were chosen and place under a co-ordinator who worked with the extension agencies and organized follow-up activity. For each cluster, five programmes were chosen each month and intensive utilization was organized around these in the selected villages. For each programme in each cluster, the co-ordinator approach an expert in the extension agency; gave him the programme synopsis in advance; collected suitable printed material ensured that the expert was in the village during transmission and that he talked to the television audience after transmission, and that he talked to the television audience after transmission, and arrange distractions, where appropriate, on the following day. During SITE about 150 village discussion of this type were held. This method proved more successful in increasing knowledge of agricultural practices among the participants than the 'television only' method used in other village nearby.

To aid utilization the science programmes for children, ISRO collaborated with he Vikram Sarabhai Community Science Center in producing a monthly wall newspaper covering the topic in the science programmes for that month plus other general science features. In addition, the teacher' notes for each programme provided synopsis, explanation of key words, and suggested per and post broadcast activities. These notes were translated into all four SITE languages and distributed to all SITE villages.

Karnik provides a their example of utilization in SITE. Since programmes on agriculture offered little to handles laborers, ISRO produced and broadcast a series on cottage industries, i.e, on making products at home with minimal invêstment and expertise for the local market. The programme aimed at motivating viewers and gave details of where to find the raw materials and how to make the products. Interested view's were invited to write for more details and received simple illustrated manuals in reply. A bank agreed to make small loans to help people to get started and later programme in the series emphasized marketing techniques. Thus utilization was aided by a comprehensive approach that touched on every aspect of helping the potential audience to set up cottage industries.

Evaluation of effects

The effects of specific programmes were first tested during production. Scripts were pre-tested by reading them aloud in villages to seen whether they contained language that was too difficult and to ascertain how much interest they evoked. Very few SITE television programmes were actually per-tested, due to pressure of time and equipment shortages. ISRO's science programmes for children were an exception; they were pre-tested , using portable half inch videotape equipment, with very useful results.

Further evaluation of effects occurred each day when one research went into each of twenty five villages to interview ten to fifteen respondents after the broadcasts. They asked the villagers which programmes they had like best, which they found most useful; they checked on villagers' comprehension of programme content; they asked about the quality of reception and how long he programmes had lasted. The researchers did this in regard to both the morning programmes for children and the evening ones for adults.

In addition, writes karnik, there were many studies of the social impact of SITE, including:

(1) a large scale longitudinal survey of social impact on adults. Carried out before, during and after SITE and governing a sample of 7,000 in twelve experiments and control villages.

(2) a study of cognitive development of school children in 122 villages together with a study of changes in their teachers;

(3) holistic anthropological studies of one village in each of six clusters carried out by researchers who lived in the villages for eighteen months, starting three months before SITE began, in order toe examine the process of rural communication before SITE, the role of television as a new medium and the process of change brought about by SITE at the local level;

(4) a message system analysis, aimed at determining what was transmitted.

ISRO carried out most of this work itself, under the eye of its own SITE social Research Co-ordination Committee, which included prominent social scientists from other institutions. A survey research Group was swept up to plan, exact and analyze the survey of adults.

Karnik Summarizes the main findings from SITE;

(1) average daily attendance per set normalized at 80-100:

(2) about 30 per cent of Indian people who had no previous contact with mass medium were reached by SITE;

(3) audiences preferred INSTRUCTIONAL programmes to pure entertainment;

(4) children's programmes were intended for those aged 5-12, but gained more than occasional viewers;

(5) those who viewers most gained most knowledge; regular viewers gained more than occasional viewers;

(6) illiterates, particularly females, gains more than literates in the area of overall modernity;

(7) a large number of agricultural innovations were triggered by the television programme, although the evidence of their ultimate success was mixed;

(8) there were substantial gains in health, hygiene and nutrition; female viewers, particularly illiterates, made dramatic gains;

(9) children watching the morning programme gained in language development and other areas. More children watched than there were registered students in the schools.

Finance

The SITE ground system was the responsibility of the Indian government, which financed it through various agencies, in particular ISRO AIR/Doordarshan and NCERT Individual states bore a further 3 per cent of costs, and UNDP bore 9 per cent. Severe ministries made contributions through the work of their extension agencies.

Mody offers a different breakdown of expenditure; she says that 82 per cent was spent on hardware, not including the satellite, per cent on software production, 3 per cent on social research and evaluation and 6 per cent on co-ordination and management. She also estimates that the project required 3,000 person/years in India.

7

Schools Broadcasting: An End of Term Report

There has certainly been a lot of broadcasting directed at formal education. Most countries have a schools broadcasting service, in some cases running continuously for over fifty years. Broadcasts have covered the whole school and in-service teacher training curriculum; every school age range has been served; and broadcasting has been used for a diverse range of teaching approaches. The output of programming for schools is probably grater today than it has ever been. But how effective is all this activity? Do teachers use it? Do pupils learn from it? What do we know about when it works and when it doesn't? What kind of report could we give on schools broadcasting?

Is there is anyone out there?

The minimum measure of effectiveness is whether or not the programmes are used in schools. No matter what the quality of the programmes, they need to be watched or heard to be effective. Since at least in Britain there is no centralised or 'core' curriculum that schools must follow, and since teachers have a good deal of freedom in how they choose to teach, it seems reasonable to assume that the programmes must have some value if teachers willingly make use of them. Cynics may argue that teachers use broadcasts because they are an 'easy option', avoiding the need a for lesson preparation, or because they 'keep the kids quiet'; even when programmes are used infaith of by teachers there is no guarantee that they will be more effective than 'ordinary' lessons. If broadcasting though is extensively used one must have a pretty jaundiced view of the whole teaching profession to assume that they are all using broadcasts as a soft option; and since most series run for at least two or three years, teachers usually have a pretty good idea of what the programmes are likely to offer. So the extent to which teachers deliberately choose to use broadcast deserves to be treated as a useful, if crude, criterion of effectiveness.

Unfortunately, though, reliable utilisation figures for schools broadcasts are available from only a few countries. In 1977 the West German International Institute for Educational Broadcasting carried out a survey of schools radio in Europe. Questionnaires were returned from 40 broadcasting organisations providing schools radio throughout twenty countries. Of the 40, only 16 had carried out or commissioned some form of audience survey of schools radio within the previous ten years. Only 7 reported regular surveys. As a result, getting an overview of the use of European schools radio is difficult. The same applies to European schools television, and the situation is even more difficult in North America where the organisation of schools television is much more fragmented than in Europe.

Fortunately though schools broadcasting in Britain is systematically monitored each year by the Educational Broadcasting Council. Table 3 sets out equipment statistics and the number of schools using broadcast services in the United Kingdom during 1981 - 82. There are several points to note from Table 3. First of all, the information is reliable, being based on a carefully drawn samples of schools with a high response rate (82 per cent). Nearly all schools have radio and television receivers and audio recorders, and most schools make at least some use of schools television and radio. While there was a slight decline in the use of radio in secondary schools from 72 per cent using at least one series in 1978 to 66 per cent in 1982, this was more than balanced by an increasing use of television. The proportion of secondary schools using television rose from 85 per cent in 1978 to 92 per cent in 1982. More significantly, the average number of series taken in each secondary school rose from 8.6 to 13.3 over that period. The increase in secondary schools using ITV series was particularly marked - from 58 per cent in 1978 to 80 per cent in 1982. This, though, did not affect the use of BBC programmes in secondary schools, the proportion of schools using their series also increasing, from 78 per cent to 90 per cent over the same period. It is probably no coincidence that this increased utilisation was paralleled by a similar rate of increase of video-cassette recorders in secondary schools - from 70 per cent in 1978 to 96 per cent in 1982.

Television and radio broadcasts are used extensively in British school. Schools using radio are likely to take an average of nine television series, and secondary schools an average of thirteen, The equipment statistics are particularly significant because while the programmes are offered without cost to the schools, the schools do have to pay for the equipment and support materials. There was a rapid increase in the purchase of colour television receivers, audio recording equipment and video- cassette recorders in schools over the five years 1978-82.

Music, dance and movement, and drama programmes for primary schools appear to be the most used radio programmes in schools, and although there are exceptions, generally the younger the age range, the grater the number of children listening to a single series. 'Let's Move', a music and movement series for the age range 5 to 6, reaches over a million school children each year, as dies 'A study by the Schools Broadcasting Council (1979) found that of the primary schools that have religious assemblies, half rely entirely on the BBC radio series. Another two music series, 'Singing Together' and 'Time and Tune', approach the million mark in terms of audiences. These four series have audiences as high as most general radio series in Britain -for instance, the audience for each episode of 'The Archers' (a popular radio serial) averages around 1.5 million.

Radio is much less used at the secondary education level, the average proportion of schools using a radio series being only 10 percent. Only two series reached more than 20 percent of secondary schools in 1982, one an advanced studies geography series for sixth formers, the other a series on electronics and micro-electronics for fourteen -to sixteen- year-old. Of the twenty-nine series made specifically for the secondary age range only twelve reached more that 50,000 pupils. Almost all secondary schools use only recording of radio programmes, and even in primary schools in 1982 the majority used recording rather than live programmes for most series.

The series with by far and away the largest schools audience in the BBC series 'Watch!', aimed at the age range 6 to 8, with more than three- quarters of the primary schools in Britain taking the series. As well as `Watch!', two other BBC series, 'Look and Read' (age range 7 to 9 +) and 'Words and Picture' have audiences estimate at over one million school children. Another eight series have audiences of over half a million,. All in the primary age ranges. Schools television series are used by about 25 per cent of secondary schools on average, although three BBC series in 1982- `Going to Work', `Scene'. And `Twentieth- Century History'- each reached .over 40 per cent of secondary schools. As with radio, the larger audiences for schools television tend to be found in the lower age ranges, due to a large extent to the increased specialisation of subject in secondary schools, leading to a grater fragmentation of the target audience.

Firstly, foreign language series are the least used on television. Even allowing for some of the series being deliberately directed at a minority audience utilisation is surprisingly low in comparison with other subject areas. For instance, although many of the science series were aimed at sixth forms, their utilisation rate is almost double that of the language series. Even on radio, secondary school language series are used by less than 10 per cent of the schools.

. Taking then the audience research figures at their face value, schools television and schools radio in Britain have both cleared the minimum evaluation hurdle: in many schools, for a side range of subject areas and age groups, extensive use is made of them.

The limitations of statistics on utilisation.

Audience figures are useful for providing a global picture of the success or otherwise of schools broadcasts. They provide useful information to broadcasting organisations on trends whether or not the use of broadcasting is increasing, or even whether a particular series over a number of years has gradually caught the interest of teachers. Audience figures can pick out particular successes or failures for series as a whole. They can be useful for justifying the use of broadcasting for schools within a broadcasting organisation of the figures can demonstrate that large numbers of children are watching or listening.

However such figures do not provide any clear indications of which educational functions or programming strategies are most appropriate for educational broadcasting. From the Educational Broadcasting Council's figures it would appear that most subject areas are suitable for treatment by television or radio. There are success and failures in each area. What we cannot tell from the audience figures is what learning has taken pace, not which of the various strategies outlined in the previous chapter have proved to be most effective.

Enrichment and learning resource

The overseas evidence

The most comprehensive review of the research in to the relative success of different strategies for educational television and radio has been carried out by Schramm. While Schramm was more concerned in that study with differences between media than with differences within a medium, nevertheless his category supplementing the formal school system closely matches the use of television and radio as a learning resource and as enrichment. His analysis of the effectiveness of these two broad strategies drew on studies of television projects in the USA, Japan, Colombia and India, and of radio in Thailand. In each of these studies there were control groups, i.e. schools or classes matched as carefully as possible, their main difference being whether or not they used the programmes.

Each one of these studies showed that students receiving television or radio as a supplement to normal teaching scored higher on the various attainment tests used than students not using the television or radio programmes. Schramm concluded:

Used as supplements to class room teaching, the media of instruction are effective. They work as well as other classroom teaching. Used in the right way, in the right place, for an appropriate purpose, they will improve the classroom experience.

A separate Japanese study, carried out by NHK, the Japanese broadcasting authority reviewed the Japanese research on schools radio during the period 1960-68. Again, comparing the performance of children who listened to schools radio with the performance of children who did not hear the programmes, they found that taking the studies as a whole:

There was little difference between classes which listened to schools radio for only on term, but after two terms or more the performance of classes who listened to the programmes noticeably increased in terms of the ability to read and write in Japanese and English, and in English the effect of listening was higher with students of higher intelligence that with those of lower intelligence.... the education effects of the broadcasts were not invariant, but depended on may factors: the quality of the programmes; the varying ability of school teachers to guide students in their use of the broadcast material; student's abilities and interests; and the length of the period of utilisation. Consequently, there were large differences from school to school on the relative effectiveness of school radio.

Both the Schramm and NHK studies clearly indicate that television and radio can lead to clear improvements when used as an enrichment or as a learning resource to supplement normal classroom activities. The NHK study, though, highlighted the fact that increased effectiveness depends on certain conditions being met, and this factor will gain increasing importance as more evidence is reviewed.

The British evidence

There is evidence from several studies that British teachers prefer to use broadcasts as enrichment rather that for direct teaching purpose. Cuff in a study of the use of a French series,' Le Nouvel Arrive', found that teachers specifically requested enrichment material. They were not interested in programmes dealing specifically with grammar. Very few teachers wanted the programmes to provide core material in a progressively structured manner throughout the year. The main desire, expressed by 62 per cent of teachers in the sample, was for material which brought the foreign country alive.

Cuff also compared classes that used 'Le Nouvel Arrive' with similar classes that did not, across six different schools. Since the main reason teachers gave for using the series was to provide background knowledge of France and the French way of life, Cuff tried to test the effects of the programmes in improving pupils' background knowledge of France. She was not able to show statistically significant gains between pupils who saw the programmes and those that did not. She argued that this was partly because pupils generally already often had good background knowledge, and also because there were only eight programmes in the series, thus giving relatively little broadcast exposure compared with other sources of information. As often happen on studies of this kind, the differences in test scores within classes were often greater than differences between classes, making it very difficult to identify any effects clearly, due to difference in treatment. Nevertheless, combining test scores and her own observation of the classes, Cuff felt confident enough to suggest that it was not so much the programmes themselves but the role played by the teacher in exploiting them which was the main determinant of whether pupils derived benefit from them. This again is consistent with the Japanese findings reported earlier. Cuff also found that teachers generally wanted more advice from the broadcasting organisation on how best to use such broadcasts.

Perhaps the most surprising result, though, given he generally poor accents of British foreign language teachers and the lack of direct exposure of British children to foreign languages outside school, was the low priority the teachers gave to the statement: 'Television can provide a wide range of native voices.' Two third of the teachers replying gave this statement a low priority for language series, and few teachers in the sample looked to television to provide a good basis for linguistic work in the classroom.

Four studies carried out by the Schools Broadcasting Council, Educational Broadcasting Council, one on the teaching of English in primary schools, one on the series 'Merry-Go-Round', one on broadcasts and project work, and one on social studies, all confirmed the preference of British teachers for broadcasting as enrichment rather than for direct teaching, across a range of subject areas and age ranges.

One project however that did come near to direct teaching was the BBC Radio series 'Listening and Reading'. These programmes were intended to develop reading skills and an interest in books, particularly for children who came from culturally impoverished home backgrounds, where the ownership and reading of books was uncommon. The broadcast programmes were intended to be taped in the schools and listened to by individual children or small groups of three or four children at the same time as following the story in the accompanying booklets, Multiple repetition was considered important, as the producer hoped that the children would want to hear and read the stories again and again. In this way, the producer hoped that the children would use listening and reading simultaneously.

The stories were read in a straightforward manner by an adult actor, with no sound effects. The undramatic style was meant to approximate to that of an adult reading intimately to a small group of children. The accompanying booklets contained texts of the programmes exactly as they were broadcast, and there was a four-page leaflet for teachers explaining the theory and principles on which the series had been planned.

The first series was used by 4,736 classes or groups,

In terms of school radio for this age range in Britain, this is comparatively low use. More importantly, few classes used the series in the way intended. In most schools, teachers used the broadcasts live because at that time the majority of infant and junior schools had insufficient recording or replaying apparatus in quantity or kind to make widespread the pioneer type of usage recommended. And consequently teachers were unable to provide any repetitions, or at best only one or two. Teachers found that only the best readers could both follow the text and listen at the same time. The rest were likely to distinguish only a few words, lose the place and then give up trying to follow. Booklets were generally in short supply for a whole class and many teachers thought that the language and vocabulary of the stories were too difficult and the reading too undramatic.

One class in each of the two schools, though, was given special treatment. Through the assistance of the National Council for Educational Technology, each school was issued with extra recording equipment and adequate copies of the booklets to enable the programmes to be used in the way intended. These two schools were also frequently visited during the series by a BBC education officer and an officer from NCERT. The two teachers involved in the scheme were asked to keep notes of pupils progress and development over the project. From the teachers reports based on two terms work, the bulletin reported that improvements were noted in the structure of the children's language, development of written work, ad spelling , and by the end of the second term, according to the bulletin, the children had developed a remarkable increase in reading power. One of the two teachers reported that, by the end of the spring term, all but six of her thirty-eight top infants could read fluently- something which had not happened in her experience in that school before.

It is clear that, when planning this series, the broadcasters did not give enough consideration to the realities of school life. Teachers in 1971 did not have the resources to work in the way intended. When the resources and support were provided, reading skills seem to have improved dramatically, but because of the way the project was setup , it is not possible to determine whether this improvement was due to the special attention given to the two schools or to the technique being tried. Given the importance of what was being attempted and the hint of what might have been achieved, it was a great pity that more consideration was not given at the time to providing support for teachers on a more wide spread scale. Closer liaison with local education authority advisers might have substantially increased the success of the project.

A rather similar study, but on a much larger scale, was carried out two year later, this time primarily on television. The main aim was to see what would be the effects if schools were provided with a reasonable and adequate level of equipment. Special efforts were made by BBC and ITV education officers and LEA advisers to help teachers in selected schools to make more effective use of schools broadcasts. In this study, 118 schools took part, and the evidence was collected in the form of unstructured, open- ended reports from teachers. This evidence, which amounted to more than two million words, was then sifted and analysed by a retired Inspector of Schools. The report suggests that given the right conditions, broadcasts clearly stimulated children's language development, imagination, and enthusiasm for using languages and this could be reasonably interpreted as further evidence of the value of broadcasts for providing enrichment and assisting teachers in the development of language skills. However, the selection of evidence from the teacher's reports is highly subjective and it is impossible to tell from the report how widespread such effects were, nor is it possible to generalise to the great majority of schools in Britain which had not been provided with extra equipment and intensive contact from broadcast education officers and local advisers, Given the unsatisfactory nature of the enquiry, it is difficult to know how much weight to give to Hayter's conclusion, but they do not seem to be too much at odds with other studies:

> When teachers were given adequate equipment and support form advisers, the value of broadcasts became fully and progressively recognised by the teachers during the course of the study.... using broadcasts well is no easy task: teachers need to be trained to make better use of broadcasting... a 'modest' increase in equipment improves considerably the perceived value of broadcasts... the existing copyright laws are a serious obstacle to better use of broadcasts in schools.

Enrichment of learning resource?

The 'enrichment' ideology is firmly held by most British educational broadcasters and their advisers. Because schools broadcasts are not didactic they allow children and teachers to respond to material in a wide variety of ways, according to the needs of individual classes, teachers and children. Using broadcasting this way enables many of the unique characteristics of television and radio- their entertainment value, their access to places, people, experiences outside the normal range of children- to be best developed and used. Broadcasters provide the resource; teachers and learners choose how to use it. This way, the autonomy of the teachers is protected. He or she is in control and not being dictated to by the broadcasters.

This is an attractive argument but one which I believe needs questioning. The distinction made in the previous chapter between 'enrichment' and 'learning resource' is important. There are quite different teaching strategies underlying these two approaches. Use of broadcasts as a learning resource suggests a more intensive and specific use- a point somewhere between the more casual enrichment approach and the more rigorously didactic approach of direct teaching. Learning resources programmes are less likely to be all thing to all men, but, where they are used successfully, their educational benefits are likely to be more profound than those of enrichment programmes.

However, there is evidence that when television or radio have been designed much more deliberately as learning resources there have been real problems. Taking all the studies as a whole, for school broadcasts to be successful, certain conditions must be met, and for learning resource broadcasts. These conditions tend to be more demanding, in that if they are not met, the programmes are more likely to fail completely. If though the conditions are met, the educational impact of learning resource programmes can be much greater than that of enrichment programmes.

Some of the necessary conditions for programmes of the enrichment and learning-resource type are indicated by the research studies:

(1) adequate provision of recording and replay equipment:

(2) more direction or suggestions to teachers on how such material might be used, specific to each series:

(3) more initial and in-service training for teachers on the use of broadcasting:

(4) adequate time to enable the full impact of a series to accumulate.

Unfortunately, there are still major difficulties that teachers often cannot overcome, even when they want to use programmes as a learning resource and are provided with adequate equipment for recording and replay. To make the most effective use of television and radio as a resource, the teacher needs to build in such material from the outset, when planning a syllabus or a project. This requires adequate information or advance warning, particularly of the programmes are to be used on transmission and not as recordings.

Secondly, only programmes classified by the broadcasting organisations themselves as educational an be legally recorded off-air in Britain. This can be particularly frustrating since so much of the material that teachers would like to use as resource material comes from general broadcasting. Until the copyright laws are changed the use of television and radio as a learning resource will continue to be limited.

It is now possible to buy or hire video- cassettes of a wide range of BBC general programmes from BBC Enterprises. However, it would cost a school about 400 to hire for instance the 13 programmes in the BBC 'Life on Earth' series just for one week. And nearly 1500 to buy them! Such pricing puts systematic use of recorded general broadcasts beyond the reach of most schools.

Despite the difficulties, some teachers are still willing to go to considerable trouble to use general broadcasts, so valuable can the material be for them. For instance, when my son was in a middle school, his teacher organised a project around the 'Life on Earth' series. It proved though to be a good example of the difficulties teachers face in using general broadcasts. Because of copying restrictions, the children working on the project were asked to watched the programmes at home- with the inevitable consequence that many children missed the programmes . Although there is an excellent book written to accompany the series, it is expensive, and written at an adult, advanced level. What would have been useful would have been a resource pack with photographs and drawing of animals and plants, and their habitats, together with suggestions for children's activities. This excellent series contains unique film, from all over the works of rare creatures an plants in their natural habitats. The programmes though were largely paid for from money raised from the British public through the license fee. It is absurd that teachers are effectively prevented from using such material in recorded from, because of copyright and cost restrictions, when the children's parents have already paid for the production costs of general programmes, through the licence fee or purchasing advertised products. Broadcasters and performers are inhibiting the use of broadcasting as learning resource material through their greed.

On the other hand, even under good conditions. The educational impact of transmitted programmes used for enrichment seems to be nebulous or marginal, providing a teachers with an 'enrichment' programme is rather like someone with be churlish to refuse, but it doesn't help much. It is difficult through to see schools broadcasters themselves moving away from programmes of the enrichment type because they reflect the same styles and approaches to programme-making found in general television and radio. Enrichment programmes also reinforce the distinction between the broadcasters role and the teachers' role . Successful utilisation of enrichment programmes is clearly seen as the responsibility of the teacher, allowing the primary activity of producers to remain making programmes.

Deliberately making educational programmes as a learning resource though requires greater attention to be paid to questions of utilisation, teacher training, linking of programmes to text books, and production styles which encourage programmes to be stopped while activities are carried out. Greater input from teachers in the design of such programmes is necessary. This though would blur the organisational boundary between broadcasting and education, and would require more in the way of resources and producer time on activities which are not so immediately and obviously related to programme-making, such as integration with text books and detailed follow-up activities.

However, the advent of video-cassettes and audio-cassettes now encourages the development of non-broadcast audio-visual learning resources. If broadcasters are unable or unwilling to develop materials for use in a learning resource mode, they may find themselves by-passed by other production agencies in the future.

Meeting special needs and deficiencies: The evidence

Despite the prevalence of the enrichment approach in British educational broadcasting, there has been very little research into how teachers make use of such material in normal working conditions, nor into its effectiveness. On the other hand, although programming for special needs is far less common, this is one of the better researched areas of British educational broadcasting, thanks largely to the IBA fellowship scheme.

Race relations

Teachers often feel unqualified, or appear to welcome assistance, when dealing with race relations within schools. Many teachers have no formal training in this aspect. Indeed, teachers often live in areas different from those in which they teach and hence have no direct experience of immigrant or ethnic communities except through the teaching context. It is fortunate then that one of the best research studies on British schools television was carried out on a Granada television series, 'Our Neighbours', aimed at the age group ten to thirteen. The researcher was an IBA Research Fellow, Graeme Kemmelfield.

The programme chosen by Kemmelfield for his study was 'Our Neighbours from Pakistan'. This showed children living in Pakistan, and a Pakistani family settling in the United Kingdom. The programme emphasised strongly the influence of the Islamic and indigenous culture on the everyday life of Pakistani families in Britain. Kemmelfield's study aimed to find out whether exposure to the programme promoted more informed understanding and sympathetic appreciation of this ethnic group. The study was as much concerned with attitude changes as with cognitive learning.

Kemmelfield used pupils in four schools in the Manchester area for the study, and there were important differences between the schools. Because previous research had shown that the density of immigrant population within areas of residence was a crucial factor in influencing the racial attitudes of Anglo-Saxin English school children. Kemmelfiedl used schools from both high and low immigrant population areas. More importantly, one of the two schools located in the high immigrant areas actually had a low proportion of immigrants in its intake. The results from this school were similar to the results from the two schools located in the low immigrant areas, whereas the results from the fourth school, the only one with a high proportion of immigrants in the intake, were quite different. In this last school, 28 per cent of the intake were of Pakistani origin, and this school was the only one which gave specific instruction on the Pakistani way of life and had a Pakistani teacher responsible for special English classes. The results from this school were consistently different from the results from the other three schools.

One result common to all four schools was that 80 per cent of the pupils 'trusted' the programme about Pakistanis, and only a small minority thought the programme was 'manipulative', by trying to change their minds about Pakistanis. In the three schools with low immigrant enrolments, the programme was not only well received by the children but was also highly effective in conveying information about Pakistani customs and ways of life. In the fourth school, while some knowledge gains were still found, these were small, since the Anglo-Saxon pupils' initial knowledge of Pakistani customs was already high.

With regard to the impact of 'Our Neighbour from Pakistan' on pupils' attitudes towards Pakistanis, the results were more complex but nevertheless important. In general, before exposure to the programme, children in the high immigrant enrolments school were more tolerant towards Pakistanis than children in the other three schools. After the programme, there was a clear increase in more favourable attitudes to Pakistanis in the three low immigrant enrolments schools, but in the fourth school, the programme led to more uncertainty in pupils' attitudes. Similarly the programme resulted in less demand for racial conformity in the three schools with low immigrant enrolments, but again caused much more uncertainty about this issue in the fourth school, where pupils had been much more tolerant of different racial customs. Also, in the three low immigrant enrolment schools, there was a tendency after the programme for more pupils to agree with statements which suggested that Pakistani children were as likeable as Anglo-Saxon English children and that the two groups should mix more together. This result was not repeated in the fourth school, where the pupils were already well familiar with Pakistani children and customs, and the programme did not affect their views on this issue one way or the other.

This study shows that programmes can change attitudes and lead to knowledge gains when there is a lack of knowledge to begin with. It also shows the highly complex ways in which pupils can react to the same programme. Kemmelfield commented that pupils responded to the programme in a relatively personal and exploratory manner and not just in terms of stereotyped group feelings and thinking. For instance, while in the three low immigrant enrolment schools there was a general shift towards accepting that cleanliness was important to Pakistanis, the same pupils reacted strongly against Pakistani eating habits, as portrayed in one particular sequence of the programme.

Kemmelfield concluded that such programmes are likely to arouse conflicting feelings and opinions in any group of children, and that, in such circumstances, the classroom teacher needs to respond with skill and sensitivity in order to make creative use of such material. Kemmelfield's research shows quite clearly the tremendous potential of television for dealing with the increasingly critical area of race relations in British schools - and also how essential it is to base such programmes on well-designed research if they are to lead to better rather than worse race relations.

Non-academic school leavers

When the school-leaving age was raised from fifteen to sixteen in Britain in 1973, teachers were faced with the challenge of providing appropriate and relevant teaching for non-academic pupils in their last year at school. The Granada TV series 'Decision' aimed to encourage school-leavers to make active, informed decisions about personal and social 'real-life' issues. Jane Steedman, another IBA Research Fellow, carried out a study of one programme in this series which dealt with buying a house. This, like Kemmelfield's, is one of the better designed studies on schools television in Britain.

An unusual feature of Steedman's study was a critical analysis of the objectives of the programme and its style in relation to its objectives of the programme and its style in relation to its objectives. Steedman's study in fact turned out to be highly critical of the programme. She found that the programme actually had the opposite effect on those who viewed it from what the programme was intended to do. The programme's overall aim was to help young people to make their own decisions and to see the relevance of certain decisions to their own decisions and to see the relevance of certain decisions to their own lives. She found though that those that viewed the programmes tended to greater conformity and acceptance of the views of 'authority figures' in the programme and to what she called 'restricted decision-making strategies' - i.e. less willingness to consider a wider range of decision option - than those who did not view the programme. For instance, the programme presented a choice of which three houses to but - but 70 per cent of the leavers lived in rented accommodation, and for these pupils Steedman claimed that a more realistic decision would have been whether or not to but at all.

Steedman claimed that the style of the programme - a documentary format, but with an authoritative and advice-giving commentary, using primarily authority figures - led to stereotyped responses to the programme and to a narrowing of the pupils' decision options. She argued that this discrepancy between programme objectives and outcome was due firstly to the teacher-adviser's original ideas for the programme - a bombardment of competing points of view - not being translated into the actual programme, and secondly to the failure of the producers of the series to analyse carefully enough what is actually involved in 'free' decision-making. She pointed out that if the aim really was to help people make their own decisions, it's best not to tell them what they should do.

Steedman's study is interesting, for a number of reasons. One reason why the programme seemed to fail was because of the producer's lack of familiarity both with the target audience and the topic, and, related to this, the failure to make the programme in the way proposed by the teacher-adviser. Secondly, the producer was clearly dealing both with a difficult topic and a difficult target group, and, in such a situation, the programme appears to have suffered from a lack of pre-production research, or at least some pre-testing, to identify the audience better and its likely response to certain topics and approaches. Lastly, the study shows the importance of the relationship between production style and programme objectives; in this case, the programme style seemed style seemed incompatible with the programme objectives.

Handicapped children

Unfamiliarity of producers with a special-target audience, failure to realise programmes along the lines originally suggested by teacher - advisers and inappropriate production styles, are also features found in some of the research into programmes used for teaching handicapped children.

This is an area fraught with difficulties for broadcasters. 'Handicapped' covers a wide range of disabilities, including severe physical or emotional handicap, children with language disorders and those with low mental abilities. Thus within the heading of 'handicap' or 'special education' he many sub-groups. Nevertheless, the total numbers are substantial. The Warnock Report on the education of children with special needs estimated that as many as 20 per cent of all school children are in need of special educational help at some stage of their school career.

Despite the difficulties with such specialised, fragmented audiences, British broadcasting organisations have transmitted several series which have been used with handicapped children. Yorkshire TV's 'Insight' was aimed at hearing-impaired and slow-learning children in the middle-school range. BBC's 'Let's Go.... was aimed at young mentally-handicapped adults, and BBC's 'Television Club' and 'Capricorn Game' are used with slow-learning children in secondary and primary schools respectively.

There have been several studies into the use of television for handicapped children. Edwards identified which programmes were used with handicapped children and how teachers adapted these programmes for use with their pupils. Porter studied slow learning children's attention to educational television programmes and the techniques which appeared to hold their attention, and Hill evaluated the 'Insight' series. Tucker investigated the perceptual requirements of blind and deaf children when using television and technical ways in which such children may be helped. Finally, Spencer and Clarke, of the University of Hull, evaluated the impact of 'Let's Go....

These research studies have been well reviewed by Proter, herself a teacher of handicapped children. She argues that from a teachers point of view, television has tremendous potential for teaching slow-learning and handicapped children. A well-designed programme can provide carefully ordered sequencing of events, controlling and organising information in ways that enable the child to comprehend what is happening, through simplifying what in the 'real' world are often complex events and processes. Similarly, programmes can carefully structure language and reinforce it with appropriate visuals. Television can provide models of how to act in certain common situations, a function particularly important for emotionally disturbed children. For physically handicapped or institutionalised children, television is particularly valuable for providing compensatory and vicarious experiences not otherwise available to them. Some of the more general characteristics of television are also important for handicapped children and carry over to educational programmes. For instance, it is often much easier to gain and hold attention through television than through other means available to the teacher. Porter points to what she calls the 'social inclusiveness' of watching television: for once, handicapped children can do what everyone else does. Lastly, Porter argues that, for handicapped children, television provides security and confidence: watching the same characters doing the same things each week is reassuring for many such children. It is also non-threatening: it never tells them off!

However, Porter claims that television is not used as much as might be expected by teachers of handicapped children. For instance, Hill found that very few schools for slow-learning children appeared to use the programmes in the 'Insight' series, a fact supported by the Educational Broadcasting Council's Annual Survey, 1979-80. From her review, Porter identified a number of reasons for television not being more heavily used in special school.

Programmes contained too much information for the children to assimilate and teachers found follow-up work difficult because individual children had focused on different information. Programmes were too fast, with too much happening on the screen and sound-track for the children to pick up the main teaching points. Handicapped children need longer to assimilate and process information than normal children; they also need constant repetition of the main teaching points. The language was too complex for handicapped children to follow and understand. Teachers often had to interpret what was said in the programmes in order to help their children understand. There was a lack of visualisation of ideas: too often most of the teaching information was given verbally. While the picture shown was actually secondary in terms of context. It should be the other way round given the large proportion of slow-learning children with language difficulties. Similarly there was often all lack of co-ordination of sound and visual channels: in frequently, the two channels did not correspond in terms of context. The handicapped child becomes confused if the verbal message does not correspond exactly with the visual information. A frequent complaint from teachers was that insufficient care was taken regarding sequencing. Edwards remarked that 'Life does not always happen in orderly sequences, but for their comprehension it needs to be presented so.' Many teachers commented on the lack of any clearly defined sequence or structural logic between the different section of the same Programme.

From her own experience as a teacher adviser to the 'Insight' series. Porter suggested several reasons for the failure of programmes for handicapped children. Producers have no experience of teaching such children, and this lack of knowledge cannot be compensated for by a few school visits and brief encounters with teachers -advisers. Even when adviser and teachers do have comments to make, these are often not implemented in the Programmes itself. 'Traditionally it has been the broadcast companies who have had control of ETV production and most educators feel that can have little real say in what is produced' Lastly, she argues that there is a lack of systematic formative research before programmes are finalised, but pre-testing is essential when dealing with such special-target groups.

With regard to this last point. It is interesting to note that 'Let's Go...' was the only one of these series tested before transmission, and pre-testing did lead to major changes in the style and tone of the transmitted programmes.

Even allowing for the very special needs of handicapped children, this research identifies perhaps more clearly than any other some of the strength and weakness of broadcasting in education in British. It is clear form these studies that British schools broadcasting has in recent years been skillful in identifying areas of special need and has tried to provide useful material for teaching in these areas. Television and radio have been used to help improve racial understanding and to teach non- academic school- leavers and handicapped children of various kinds. In all the cases examined. The studies confirmed the huge potential of television and radio for providing substantial help in what teachers themselves recognise to be difficult areas.

The research has also shown that such programmes require great care and preparation. In particular, very accurate knowledge of the target audience is necessary. Kemmelfield highlighted the complex ways in which pupils reacted to a programme and the consequent need for the classroom teacher to respond with skill and sensitivity if the impact of the programme was to be creatively harnessed. Steedman found that the programme she studied failed because the nature of the target audience and how decision are actually made were not fully understood by the production team. The studies on programmes for handicapped children also suggest more failure than success, again due to inadequate knowledge of the target audience and a failure to take into consideration in the design of programmes the special needs of such children.

It is of course because such areas are difficult that television and radio can be so useful to teachers. However, broadcasting will only be useful if the programmes actually help the teacher and tackle the problems effectively.

Once a series has been decided on by the Advisor Committee to the various broadcasting organisation. He then visits a few and talks to a few teachers and possibly consults some books an other programmes. Then the producer, after consultation with other production colleagues, prepares a script an produces the programme. It is then previewed by senior production colleagues an possibly by an education officer, and then transmitted. It seems though that, at least for programmes which are intended to meet special needs, the conventional production process is inadequate. Much closer teacher involvement, and, above all, adequate formative research before finalising the programme, appear to be essential. Programmes aimed at meeting special needs then are likely to require more resources and a longer production period, and to be more demanding on producers than the usual schools broadcast. It is a high-risk area but one where broadcasting could be particularly valuable for education. Period that broadcasters are willing to change their current approach.

Direct teaching and curriculum reform: success at a price

While exhaustive research on educational broadcasting in developed countries is very rare, the use of broadcasting for direct teaching in developing countries has been extensively researched.

Most of these evaluations have been based on comparative measurements of performance, either before and after the introduction of the new system, of between pupils covered by the projects and pupils receiving conventional education. Many of the studies provide details cost analyses and general data on the countries economic, social and educational development problems. Schramm has collected together and analysed the research evidence from several of these projects, and Arnove presents an excellent critique of the use of television for educational reform and development in developing countries, drawing on several of these studies. Consequently , I wish here to concentrate on some of the broader issues.

Signals were to be bounced off reflectors attached to the balloons, providing national coverage for both educational television an radio programmes which were to be used as the badis of a new, reformed school curriculum. However, the balloons proved to be aerodynamically unstable. The American Westinghouse Corporation, the main contractors, agreed as compensation to provide equipment for a more conventional ground-based system. However this delayed the opening of the educational radio and television networks from 1976 to 1981. In the meantime, the curriculum reform went ahead, with the result existing curriculum, rather than for direct teaching.

Taking the studies as a whole the use of broadcasting for direct teaching and curriculum reform has on balance led to substantial educational improvements in the countries concerned. The improvements took several forms:

(1) increased enrolment in the formal school system; for instance, in the El Savador project, enrolments is grades 7-9 increased from 20,000 at the start of the reform to 65,000 within five years:

(2) reduced drop-out after enrolment: for instance, in Niger, those pupils included in the scheme continued their schooling right through the five primary grades, with virtually no drop- outs; in El Salvador, of those who entered the seventh grade in 1970, 91 per cent continued into the ninth grade in 1972, compared with 68 per cent in 1969:

(3) educational standards, as measured by objective performance tests, were raised; in Nicaragua at all grades covered by the scheme, pupils taught mathematics by radio learned more then pupils taught in traditional classrooms, and these results were consistent across different types of school and levels of ability; in ETV Maranhao, ETV students achieved higher pass rates on public examinations than students from conventional private schools, although students in the ETV schools generally came from poorer families;

(4) on some projects, costs per student for broadcast based direct teaching projects were estimated to the lower than the costs for traditional education without deterioration of educational standards; costs for instance for the Telesecundaria system have been estimated to be 25 per cent less than costs for an equivalent conventional provision in EI Salvador, by 1973. The cost per student using ETV was estimated to be about 10 percent lower than the cost per student had ETV not been used class size not increased and teaching load not changed.

Increased enrolments longer schooling improved standards at no greater costs than those found in conventional teaching, are substantial achievements. Such performance would be welcomed by many governments even in developed countries; given the difficulties that had to be overcome in the developing countries where these scheme have been introduced the achievements are remarkable. While one con quibble over some of the results, it is clear that direct teaching through broadcasting has substantially improved educational provision in several developing countries, within reasonable cost limits.

Nevertheless, doubts remain. Educational standards in some of these countries were appealingly low at the time of the introduction of the television or radio reform. Had the same amount of manly bed invested steadily in the conventional education system over a regular period of time the need for major reforms might not have arisen in the first place.

Where foreign aid has been provided through a bilateral agreement it usually covered mainly capital costs of for buildings and equipment, such as the construction of a studio complex and transmitters and production and transmission equipment. Such bilateral aid was rarely in the form of an outright grant, so both capital and interest had to be repaid eventually, even if at less than market rates of interest. Often such aid was tied to the purchase of equipment and services from the loaning country. As the example from Afghanistan shows, initial equipment may be purchased at discount prices with the help of low-interest inter-governmental loans. However, the developing country then finds that the initial investment its insufficient to maintain or develop and adequate service; nevertheless, necessary subsequent purchases - often far exceeding the original investment- must be paid for at full cost in scarce foreign currency, usually through further loans negotiated at full market interest rates. Thus the developing country becomes reliant on foreign technology and loans, and the cycle of dependency and debt is strengthened.

International aid agencies, such as the World Bank and the United National Development Programmes, have generally been cautious in funding educational broadcasting projects which give the developing country more chance of obtaining direct economic gains from the investment.

Several developed count tries run training courses in educational broadcasting for which grants or bursaries are available from these countries and from international aid agencies. Again though training in well maintained, expensive and highly sophisticated Western production centers, in a foreign language is not always appropriate.

In the projects evaluated, though the main problems have arisen when the foreign assistance has ended. It has often proved difficult for the developing country to maintain a high standard of teaching and to integrate the projects into the main education system. The running costs of such projects is -pupils worksheets, teachers manuals, transport costs, salaries for production, technical and administrative staff, the costs of

TV or radio receivers, and the maintenance and replacements of equipment - are rarely alone can far exceed the total of foreign capital aid. The national government then had to find large amounts of money, skilled manpower and administrative effort to continue such projects and several countries have found it impossible to maintain adequate services over a long period.

Many of the projects have been pilots' or experiments.

In such cases it has been impossible to assess the full economic costs and benefits or the operational difficulties or using broadcasting for direct teaching on a large-scale or continuous basis. Indeed,. there is a disturbing tendency for developing countries to be used as yes-beds for advance technological applications that developed countries themselves have not been prepared to use extensively as witnessed by the South Korean and Indian satellite projects.

There are also doubts about the emphasis placed on television lather then radio on such projects. Two of the three countries that have used television for direct teaching and curriculum reform on a national scale, American Samoa and EI Salvador are both small compact countries easily covered by a television transmission system and most schools are within easy reach of highways and electricity supplies. In the third country the Ivory coast considerable efforts had to be made to provide schools with suitable reception equipment. Special battery operated sets suitable for the French SECAM system, had to be designed and a sophisticated and costly maintenance system established. The Indian satellite project was restricted to villages with mains electricity supplies. It is extremely expensive to provide television sets for schools on a national basis, particularly if local generators have to be supplied where there is no mains electricity.

Radio on the other hand can operate on low-powered low-cost batteries. Furthermore while television is becoming much more widespread in Latin America and some South-East Asian countries, there are still many developing countries where the television signals cover only the main urban areas. Whereas medium and short-wave radio transmitters usually give a national coverage.

It is though the poor rural areas where television does not reach which usually have the most inadequate educational provision. Television production, maintenance and distribution all require grater numbers of higher qualifies staff than radio, providing a drain on scarce technical manpower from other possible development activities. Television because of the high technical standards demanded' also carries a much greater risk than radio of breakdown or failure. Radio then would appear to have several advantage over television for very poor countries apart form in Nicaragua though radio has not been used for direct teaching and curriculum reform.

The financial implication and the relative value of radio compared to television are general concerns for the use of the broadcasting in developing countries. There are also concerns specific to its use for direct teaching. The first concern is a practical one. Direct teaching by television or radio requires large amount of production and transmission time. At one stage the American Samoa project which introduced a whole television based curriculum for all primary grades in one year and all secondary grades in the next was producing 6000 live programmes a year. This meant programmes makers were making twenty programmes each per week. It is difficult to disagree with Schramm's comment that 'the enormous load of love programming must have had an effect on the quality of the broadcast's! In EI salvador a production team was responsible for making three television programmes a week. This still system over a twelve hour studio day to get enough programmes made in time. The Nicaraguan project required the production of between three and five radio lessons a week, for one subject alone. Most of the projects introduced direct teaching for one year-level or grade at a time, and ,specially when formative evaluation was used the programmes once finalised were recorded and used again in subsequent years. Even so production loads still tend to be heaving comparison with developed countries. For instance at the Open University, producers make only six to ten educational television programmes a year.

Furthermore, such production requirements even when spread over a one grade per annum, have a cumulative effect on transmission times. Five radio or television Programmes a week each of 30 minutes length require 2 and 1/2 hours transmission time for one grade and one subject. To cover six grades, 15 hours a week would be required for one subject. Given that there are limited time during the day when programmes can be broadcast to schools it would be difficult on one channel to accommodate more than two subjects over six grades.

A different concern is the educational limitation of direct, centralised teaching. While some subjects like mathematics which may have common standard learning objectives, may lend themselves more to direct teaching other subject areas do not. For instance, development of communication skills such as language and imaginative writing demands more individual and less' convergent' responses from learners and consequently far grater interaction with the teacher and other children in the class. Above all though direct teaching ignores the social role of education. Teaching is not just about the transfer of information and the development of common cognitive skills. Many educators see personal relationships and social contact as an integral part of the educational process. It is a legitimate concern that educational media and in particular direct teaching through television and radio could lead to narrow mechanistic instruction more suited to robots than to children. Furthermore, loading the whole curriculum on to television or radio means that the media cannot be used selectively, concentrating on those teaching function for which they are more suited and leaving other functions to book's or personal interaction between teachers and children.

It will also probable come as no surprise to learn that some of the direct teaching projects ran into trouble with teachers. In EI Salvador after a favorite start the teachers showed increasing hostility towards the television reform which culminated in a two month strike; the telesecundaria teachers in Mexico had running battle with educational authorities for a more appropriate job classification and better salaries.

Lastly Lyle in looking back on the development of a number of television and radio projects first reported in 1967 noticed the movement of many of the original projects form direct teaching to using television and radio to supplement or enrich the work of the classroom teacher. He also noted that the more control teachers had over how and when to use television material the grater the chance of its utilisation. He also commented that the provision of material on cassettes greatly increase the control that teachers have which in turn leads to greater utilisation of television material a point noted earlier with regard to schools television in Britain.

It is however too sample to dismiss direct teaching through broadcast television as an inferior form of education. In many developing countries conventional teaching is mechanical based on rote-learning and accurate recall of fact or procedures which are often totally irrelevant to the children and the society in which they live. Teachers are often barely more educated than the children they are teaching; the teachers will have received littl. instruction in either educational theory or practice, they will have very few resources such as text books or equipments at their disposal. The provision of cassette machines is out to the question for many of the poorer countries. In such circumstances direct teaching through television and radio may not only be more directly effective but can also provide appropriate models of teaching for them teachers. Teachers hostility has been due less to direct teaching and more to poor working conditions and low salaries. In EI salvador teachers had to take larger classes and work longer hours with no increase in salary. In Mexico the Telesecundaria teachers were drawn from primary schools but despite teaching at a secondary school level, they were being paid led that conventional secondary school teachers. In other direct teaching projects such as Nicaragua more care was taken with the teachers.

Direct teaching in fact does not necessarily mean that social learning and group work are excluded. Most direct teaching by television or radio is followed by periods where pupils and teachers work together in more conventional ways, reinforcing and developing material contained in the programmes. The ETV Maranhao project indeed is structured so that there is a great deal of social interaction per-group dynamics and pupil leadership. Each group elects a leader and a rapportuer on a monthly, rotating basis. After each programme, students work individually or in groups of six of seven. Group leaders are expected to pose questions or suggest activities to be carried our by individuals in the groups. Although there are monitors, these are not qualified teachers, and each monitor covers several groups. Thus the systems depends on a good deal of discipline from the secondary pupils. Oliveira reports that although discipline problems exist, they are fewer than in conventional school in Brazil.

One major reservation about this use of broadcasting in education stems from unease about the political motivation behind such projects, rather that from doubts about the political motivation behind such projects, rather that from doubts about their educational effectiveness in terms of performance and costs. They can easily be seen as palliatives for problems which need much more radical solutions. It is exceedingly dangerous to think that even a massive injection of external finance and technical assistance for broadcast-based curriculum reform will make much of a dent of the problems of developing countries. For instance, five years after the first group of students had progressed entirely through the new system in El Salvador, I watched on my television set news film of government troops shooting done those very students on the steps of the cathedral in San Salvador. Whatever else the most throughing attempt to use television for national curriculum reform may have achieved, it did not tough the underlying social and economic problems of El Salvador. Such projects cannot substantially compensate for the problems caused by poverty, inequitable distribution of wealth, oppressive government and unequal international trade relations.

For politicians and administrators though who have to work with the existing socio- economic framework of their country, direct teaching by television- or better still by radio- is still clearly an option worth considering. Direct teaching by television and radio can assist curriculum reform, can increase enrolments and an raise educations, standards, at possibly lower cost than conventional alternatives. To do this, however, very demanding conditions have to be met, and the long-with financial implications can be serious. Lastly, adequate long-term national financing is essential, and the teachers ultimately will need to feel that they have control over when and how television and radio are to be used if the innovation is to survive and lead to long-standing educational improvements.

Evaluating broadcasting in the formal school system is not helped by the unevenness of research. While there has been extensive evaluation of the use of broadcasting for curriculum reform in developing countries, the vast majority of schools broadcasting in Europe and North America has been unresearched. A good deal of the research that has been carried out on school broadcasting has been amateurish, or focused on a very narrow range of information, such as providing utilisation statistics or identifying the possible audience for likely new series. There has been very little research into what can best be learned through television or radio, into the most effective ways of designing programmes to meet specified learning objectives, or into the programme design requirements for specialist target audiences. Although formative research is an important component of the Agency for Instructional Television's approach in the USA, this is an exception in schools broadcasting. Many of the programmes in Britain that have been systematically researched after transmission were seen to have suffered from a lack of formative research., There was for instance often inadequate understanding of the abilities or needs of target groups and mistaken assumptions about the likely responses to the programmes. Although again there exceptions, in most countries the broadcasting organisations are largely responsible for the lack of research. Few have carried out research themselves into the learning impact of schools broadcasts. The main exceptions are AIT in the USA, the Swedish Educational Broadcasting Company and the IBA in Britain, through its fellowship scheme, though even this needs to be strengthened through better research training and supervisor for the fellows, most of whom are seconded schoolteachers. Broadcasting organisations have also done little to encourage universities to research into this area. Regular contacts between university departments and broadcasters over a continuous period are needed if university-based research is to be relevant, appropriately designed and useful. Research is needed not only to help broadcasters to make more effective programmes, but also to help teachers and teachers trainers to make better use of broadcasting in the schools.

It is a great pity that more research has not been done. The lack of research makes evaluation difficult but, more importantly, research, when it has been carried out professionally and in collaboration with broadcasters, has often indicated what needs to be done to improve the effectiveness of programmes.

Despite the lack of research, several conclusion can be drawn. Firstly, broadcasting can be and has been used effectively for a wide range of purposes in the formal education system. Secondly, in Britain at least, school broadcasting is very extensively used by teachers and pupils. Indeed, there is probably greater use today of television broadcasting in British schools than at any time previously. Teachers in Britain clearly prefer programmes that enrich and supplement their teaching. It has been difficult to find evidence in Britain that this kind of programming has had much direct effect on learning, although studies overseas have been more positive.

One reason for the growing use of television in British school is the increasing availability of video recording and playback facilities. These facilities also make it possible for programme materials to be used much more specifically and effectively as learning resources, more fully integrated with and central to the teaching than enrichment programming. This approach in schools though is still comparatively rare, and require different programme design strategies, provision of adequate recording and playback equipment , easier access to and better knowledge of pre-recorded material, and better training of teachers in the use of media as learning resources. Copying restrictions on general programming are a major obstacle to greater use of television as a learning resource. These restrictions make it virtually impossible to use general programming legally in schools. Despite a recent report for the government has chosen to ignore completely the educations. Issue regarding copyright of broadcast television programmes. It is not surprising therefore that there is a good deal of illegal use of general programmes in schools.

The research indicates that television could also play a vital role in meeting special needs within schools but it rarely manages to do so. Programme strategies are not usually adapted to the learning needs of such special target groups. Formative research, essential to successful programme- making in this area, is usually not done Producers have often failed to make sufficient and appropriate use of specialist advice. This is a high-risk area, requiring greater skill and resources for often smaller audiences , but an area where broadcasting could make a major contribution to the formal school system.

Direct teaching by broadcasting is found almost exclusively in developing countries. When used in this way, television and radio have been associated with clear improvements in the educational service. However, for such projects to be successful, very demanding conditions have had to be met. Although direct teaching projects have been successful in performance terms, there are still considerable doubts about their wider educational, economic and political implications.

In contrast, there seems to be less controversy about the value of television and radio for in-service teacher training. Large number of teachers- in both developed and developing countries-have received further education and training through these media. Quite often, though, broadcasting is only a part- and sometimes a minor part-of multi-media courses for teachers. Moreover, teachers are already well-educated and so have probably developed sufficient learning skills to be successful independent learners. They are often also highly motivated to success through such courses, since successful completion usually leads to higher qualifications, higher statue and higher pay.

It can be seen then that television and radio can be successfully used for a wide variety of purposes, in a wide variety of contexts. However, in order for broadcasting to be used successfully, certain conditions must be met. Many of these conditions- such as the motivation of the target group, training of teachers in the use of media, the availability of equipment - lie outside the programmes themselves. The use made of formative research and specialist advisers- are very much under the direct control of programme producers. There is a good deal of evidence to suggest that the conditions necessary for effective programming in this are frequently not met, although in Britain at least, the programmes are heavily used. An end-of -term report on school broadcasting then might be: 'Should not be misled by the apparently good performance so far. Could do much better- and will need to given nest term's challenges.

8

Should Children Still Listen

Can you imagine your family settling down in the evening and tuning in a favorite drama on the radio console? After all, not so very long ago radio was a primary source of stories for both children and adults. Youngsters in the 1940s locked forward to hearing the latest episode of such shows as The Lone ranger, The Shadow and Our Miss Brooks. What happened?

These days when the family settles down in the evening, some from of video most likely furnishes the fantasies. Children in the 1980s anticipate seeing their favorite shows on television, cable, or on video cassette.

Not that radio has disappeared from our lives. Far from it. There are more radios in America today than televisions and telephones combined. Count the radio in your house. But radio listening has changed. Physically, radio are smaller, more portable, and specially equipped for solo listening. Mysteriously wired pedestrians, bicyclists and bus passengers move to rhythms only they and their Walkman can hear. Radio now offers deferent program content too. Even with dramatic productions from Children's Radio Theater, The Web, New Waves and others, there is little fiction for children available on the air.

Children listening today can find music, not melodrama. But music listening presents fewer demands than listening to drama or prose. Music purists may disapprove, but most people us radio music as a backdrop for accomplishing other things.

Should three b radio fiction for children? Perhaps its scarcity speaks the truth all too loudly; if radio stories were appealing or important enough, they would persist. Why would youngsters with ready access to illustrated tales choose strictly aural ones? With television setting children's standards for fiction, pictures must seem mission more by accident than design. Telling stories on radio may also seem old fashioned to the young. Commercial radio broadcasters voice skepticism about the economic viability of programming for children in general. Audience rating services ignore the under-twelve listener.

But maybe the radio broadcasters' doubts are unwarranted. According to one knowledgeable source, 'There's every indication from parents and kinds that there's a real audience for children's radio, But we've given it a real chance. You need a block of good programs and lots of money for promotion. Today's compact radios and earphones allow for such intimate listening. Whether amid a crowded street or under the covers in bed, modern radio and audio cassettes might set a wonderful stage for the most personal storytelling - where children's own visions of the world can prevail.

This chapter examines the educational evidence for a

against having children within earshot of audio fiction. Are children losing out on a learning experience by not listening any more?

What children miss, listening

'Listen and attend,' invites a story record narrator in her friendliest voice. But make no mistake about it: that means work. A young listener must keep up with the passing flow of words, yet has no control over their speed. And even when listening to an ideal rate of speech, sustaining attention to an unseen voice takes concentration. What is there to look at? What are your hands supposed to do? Young listeners also must make sense of what they hear and reconstruct a meaningful message in their own mind. No wonder listening to recorded prose leaves so many young children restless and bored, or asleep. Youngsters who grew up with radio must have faced the same problems; yet its stories managed to capture their attention and loyalty.

The demands of story listening take their toll. Researchers comparing different versions of the same story find children neither remember nor understand radio fiction as well as they do that in illustrated books or on television. Young listeners include more wrong information retelling a radio story and answer fewer factual questions correctly. Note, however, that what these investigators call 'radio' is often just a recorded reading of a story, rather than a full dramatization.

Having to rely on words alone limits children's story understanding. With no additional cues from pictures, sound effects, or music, children may be unable to decipher new words or complex sentences. Admittedly, hearing words in context does offer clues to their meaning. To astute young listeners, the sentence: 'Then filled the doll's bowl with pounded yams' may suggest yams are something to eat. But this clue is available in other media versions as well. Hearing words with expression also may help explain them. In the 'yams' case, however, even trying to make them sound delicious in no way reveals their identity. The more key words and phrases children miss, listening, the less their grasp of and interest in the text.

Oral stories also present problems when children reason beyond the given text. To understand a story in any medium requires making all kinds of inferences, from the grammatical to the logical. A well-organized story presents information where it is needed, but it is still up to the individual to infer how these words and actions are related. Only then is a narrative coherent. Such reasoning begins right from the opening lines, as in this example from a Grimms' fairy tale, The Fisherman and His Wife:

> There was once a poor fisherman who lived with his wife in a tiny hut by the sea. Each morning he went down to the shore and cast his net for fish. One day he pulled up a fish with gold a silver scales.

Having the first two sentences in mind, we readily deduce in the third who pulled up the fish, how, when, and where. Young children make relatively easy connections like this too. But the farther apart two story events, the more difficult it becomes for children to relate them, such as connecting a character's motive with the behavior it causes.

Radio calls on audiences to contribute more inferences. Listeners do more work filling in between the lines than most other story audiences. Even the simple reasoning above is eliminated for young TV viewers, who actually see the fisherman retrieve the fish on screen. The television picture delivers story evidence which otherwise must be inferred.

More spare story media like radio also leave fewer clues on which to base inferences. Not always is the relevant information right there in the text, as in the preceding example. This becomes especially evident when children use inferences to elaborate their knowledge of story characters, actions and settings. What kind of guy is this fisherman, anyway?

Young listeners import more outside information than viewers to answer this kind of question. Visualizing the fisherman, radio listeners know at this point only that he is poor. At least that helps some nine-and ten-year-olds with costuming; they proceed to picture him in patches and ragged clothes. But there are so many details of physical appearance to account for. How old is he, for instance? Young viewers can refer to such telltale signs of age as hair color, whiskers and wrinkles. Without pictures, specific voice cues, or text, young listeners seek evidence elsewhere: they bring to bear personal experience and world knowledge, such as it is. But children's experience is limited, and it sometimes leads them to draw idiosyncratic or stereotyped conclusions from their listening. Thus we find errors in children's comprehension of radio stories.

Bottom-line story listening

What young listeners do remember from oral stories, demanding though they may be, reflects an uncanny sense of narrative form. Children retelling an oral story, one short and simple enough to be within their grasp, intuitively include the most important information and omit many minor details. First graders typically mention at least one main character, an even that initiaties the story, and the consequence that finally results. Other content, such as characters' reactions and attempts to reach a goal, gets added as the audience matures.

Here is what one seven-year-old boy told me, recapitulating the African folktale A Story a Story about the origin of stories on earth:

The guy wanted to have the stories.

And then the king in the sky said he has to pay and get all like a tiger and bees and a fairy that-no-man-has-seen.

So he got'em. Then he spinned a web and brought them back to the king of the sky.

Then he got all the stories and brought them back to his village.

This is bottom-line story recall. With great economy of means, he volunteered just enough information to recreate the bare bones of the story.

Where do children get their narrative savvy? For one thing, stories identify themselves by conforming to a certain starchier or plan: a text needs a setting, beginning, development and resolution to qualify as a story. Children construct an analogous mental map of story structure based on their exposure to literature. They come to expect fictional events to proceed in a prescribed manner as well - the hero will succeed in his mission, the villain will ultimately fail. The younger children are, the stronger their preference for stories organized that way.

Children also learn about fiction from firsthand experience. Cause and effect relationships, essential to fiction, are tested all the time in real life; if I misbehave and pull my sister's hair, will I be caught and punished? Children use what they understand about the world to evaluate the credibility of story characters, settings and events.

Young listeners' mental schemes for narratives help them organize a story as they hear it. The more a story conforms to this ideal or at least expected form, the better children remember it. When elementary school students hear a story out of order, they tend in their own accounts to reorganize events in standard sequence. Children will try and make narrative sense out of scrambled picture sequences too. Children's as well as adults' memory for stories simply gravitates towards the course of events to which they are accustomed.

Robust as young children's basic story scheme is, it is something they don't consciously apply. Second graders perform poorly, at any rate, when asked to sort out story content in terms of its relative importance. Later, when children are formally taught the rigors of story form, they discover what, in a nascent sense, they already know.

The sound of language

The memorability of oral stories does not depend solely on reliable structure or even on meaningful content. Another secret of oral literature's longevity, the one most germane to radio, is the way that it sounds in our ears. Traditional storytellers, film, television and theater, have in common with radio the power to impart sonic beauty to their verbal message. But sound matters more to radio than to any audiovisual medium. Most ephemeral of all, radio storytellers cannot speak to their audience in person or been in the flesh; only the relayed sound of their voices can be heard.

Spoken stories exploit the sound of language several ways. Among the most basic phonetic features oral literature employs is repetition. Alliteration, rhyme and refrain all depend on sound repetition for their effect, whether at the level of letter, word or phrase. Meter and rhythm are based on repeated patterns of sound and syntax. It is raining' merely delivers weather information, whereas 'It is raining, raining, raining' is a more emphatic, rhythmic and expressive message. Preference also may be given to words whose sounds suggest their meaning: 'callous' characterizes a hardened person better than the softer sounding 'insensitive.' Onomatopoeic words resemble even more closely the sound of their referents - try 'splash,' 'bang,' or the more delicate 'plop.' Appropriate use of language's sensuous qualities elevates a story text from the prosaic to the poetic.

Children tend to remember poetic language in stories they hear. The very words and phrases that use sound to advantage - despite their marginal importance to the plot - appear often in young listeners' accounts.

The sound of story language has greater impact on children when it is not competing with moving pictures. Radio narration elicits better recall of poetic or flavorful vocabulary than does a cartoon version of the same text; compared to viewers, school age listeners correctly identify more of a story's onomatopoeic sounds, and elaborative phrases. Listeners more often refer to characters by their formal names, 'Ananse the spider man,' whereas viewers make vague references to 'the man' or just 'him.' Even preschoolers, notorius for their brief story descriptions, include more specific wording after a strictly auditory delivery; listeners report: 'The whale ate every fish in the sea,' whereas viewers simply say, 'He ate all the fish.' Once children see stories on television or film, as I later discuss, pictures become more important than words.

How aware children are of a story's use of words is debatable, however. On one hand, research indicates children pay more attention to what happens in a story than how it is told. Preschoolers will complete in identical fashion stories of similar content but opposing moods: whether the protagonist was thrown overboard in a storm or jumped overboard for a swim in the sun, he is invariably returned to his boat and sent home to bed. Elementary school children asked to pick a consistent continuation for a story or poem will base their choices more on verbal content than on style. After hearing this opening passage:

> How pleasant to know Mr. Peer!
> Who has written such volumes of stuff!
> Some think him ill-tempered and queer,
> But a few think him pleasant enough

more students follow up with a verse further describing Mr Peer than one using a consistent thyme pattern.

> (a) Here's a man who's very nice indeed,
> I'd like to have a book of his to read.
> Sometimes, it's true, he starts to lose his temper.
> Yet Mr Peer is pleasant each November.

> (b) She sits in a beautiful parlor,

With hundreds of tiles on the wall;
She drinks a great deal of Marsala,
But never gets tipsy at all.

On the other hand, children's language sensitivity may not be tapped by such rigorous tasks. For instance, young listeners will sometimes continue a story with phrases they like the sound of, regardless of whether they agree in style with the previous text. Perhaps their sense of story language, like that of its structure, is only intuitive. In that case, young listeners reveal their appreciation of poetic language by repeating its rhymes and refrains, and by asking to hear again stories that use such vocabulary.

Listening to radio drama

Listening involves attending to so much more than language. Yet we routinely equate listening comprehension with knowledge of word meanings and take for granted the significance to children of sounds - shrieks, screeches, crashes, creakings, weepings, whispers, roars, rustlings, tweets, tinkles, slaps and sighs. Only in music class are children credited with having an ear for more than semantics. Radio drama takes advantage of sound quality in several ways, the most basic of which is having each character speak his or her own part.

Voice: The mental image we conjure up listening to a radio voice can be so vivid that actually seeing the person behind the microphone is surprising or downright disappointing. An actor's tone of voice lends shades of meaning typically lost in print. It helps establish a character's sex, age, mood, even physical stature. Speech accent and dialect suggest social class and nationality. A radio character's voice carries critical dramatic weight; a speaker silent too long is forgotten.

Children rely on the way people's voices sound to interpret an audio drama. Elementary school students will use characters' accents to establish the setting for a radio episode: 'I think the story happened in England because of the way they talk.' Accent, more than any other clue, helped them, correctly infer this drama's location. Nine and ten-year-olds will base a hero's size on his voice: 'I think he's small,' ventured one boy, 'because of the way he talks - he has a small voice'. I have even heard fifth graders determine a character's physical state from his breathing: 'Owl was tired of flying, he was taking deep breath.' Children's attention to voice is scattered throughout my media research at Harvard. This is suggestive evidence, however.

But the impact voices have on children is also common knowledge. Infants respond differently to angry shouts than to soothing whispers before they know what the respective words mean: to which remark will an infant react more cheerfully, 'I love you' spoken in a loud gruff voice or 'I hate you' said in a soft caressing tone? Toddlers comply less often to a command delivered as a thin, hesitant plea. Without dramatic coaching, adults adjust their voices to make certain impressions on children. Among radio actors, achieving such effects is a profession.

Sound effects Cockadoodledoo! A single sound can bring an entire scene to mind if it is charged with unmistakable associations. Sound effects are an integral part of radio drama production. One producer explains:

> 'Door closes' looks simple enough on the page. But how is the door to be closed? Is the character striding out of the room in a fury? If

> so the door needs to be banged. Or is the creeping out? If so it must be closed quietly and carefully. And how soon after the line should we hear the door? Points like this go to the heart of a play's credibility.

A radio producer's careful handling of sound is not lost on children. In one Harvard study, children ages eight through twelve identified sound effects compiled on audiotape. Many subtle sound qualities emerged in their descriptions. Hearing a door open and close, then footsteps growing fainter, one third grader said: 'Someone's slamming a door and walking away inside a hall.' Notice her attention to how the door was closed, to the pace and direction of footsteps, even to the acoustical background.

Children associate sound effects with characters' actions, props and surroundings. Listening to the radio episode of Treasure Island, youngsters inferred a wintry scene 'because you could hear the wind blow,' knew the captain was in a crowded tavern 'because of the glasses and people talking in the background,' and that he paid for his drink in coins 'because you could hear them clinking.' Sound effects provide children with aural images of story content; omitting them is like removing a radio story's illustration.

Children this age also can judge whether a given sound belongs in a story. They sorted out among the sound effects on tape which ones were plausible and which inappropriate to include in this Treasure Island broadcast: yes, horse hoofbeats belonged; no, car traffic did not.

The younger children are likely, and the more limited their vocabulary the more likely they are, to depend on sounds to follow an aural narrative - with one obvious but critical caveat. Younger children's repertoire of familiar sounds is more limited as well. Sound effects must be within listeners' experience to be effective. A child must have heard a sound before and be able to recognize it without seeing its source; for example, the identity of an old wheelbarrow rattling down the road went undetected among this youthful urban audience. Interpreting a busy soundtrack is like an informative mystery game, providing the clues are meaningful to the players listening.

Music Even babies respond to the moods music evokes. The calming effect on infants of softly sung lullabies is familiar to parents worldwide. Six-month-olds can recognize simple melodies and rhythms. By age eight or nine, children have the musical ability of untrained adults.

No wonder then, that eight- to twelve-year-olds interpreted music in the Treasure Island broadcast with such sensitive ears. Most children described as happy an upbeat sea chanty, for example, whereas an eerie synthesizer passage sounded spooky and scary. No one confused the two effects. Music offered older children clues to story setting as well; a sailor song at one point suggested pilgrims, England, and the sea. Listeners discounted the non-Western sound of a percussive African rhythm as unsuitable for this story.

What makes music so expressive for children? First there is the distinctive way a piece of music sounds. Music is composed of several elements: pitch, melody, modality, rhythm, harmony, dynamics, tempo and timber. Each musical element contributes to the overall emotional tone. According to adults judges, speeding up a piece makes it more exciting or gay; slowing it down can sadden, dignify, or calm its mood. Children perceive these differences too. Some tunes just sound more cheerful to them than others.

Children also acquire emotional responses to music. Treasure Island's music reminded many children of past experiences with similar-sounding music: the sea chanty was reminiscent of carnivals and circuses, the synthesizer of ghost stories and horror movies. As children get older, their musical associations grow more plentiful, their ears more attuned to our culture's popular musical genres and harmonies. With a flick of the radio dial most American teenagers can tell where their music loyalties lie. Audio productions can make good use of music young listeners already know and enjoy; the right opening tune can entire them into radio drama before any action takes place.

Finally, music heard in the context of radio drama has the story itself working in its favor. Although usually lacking its own subject matter, music can be composed or selected to do particular narrative work, such as defining a character or mimicking his movement. Which instrument sounds more like a fat person's footsteps, as tuba or a flute? Think of Prokofiev's Peter and the Wolf. The specific settings, characters and actions a story supplies must help children appreciate the flavor of m accompanying music, just as music informs the accompanying verbal message.

The detection dilemma Medium effects on children's story learning often elude our notice. Younger listener's responsiveness to sounds is a perfect example.

The problem rest in part with audience perception.

Background music, especially when continuous, often influences listener's feeling or ideas about a story without their realizing it. This lack of awareness is frequently the desired outcome. Music, sounds effects, acoustic background, even internals of silence, are expected to contribute unobtrusively to a radio drama's overall impact. The effects of such auditory features are even more subtle for young children, who know little about their production.

Nor are children trained to base story inferences on nonverbal sound clues. I have rarely heard children mention music retelling a story, even when they know its songs by heart. Sound-inclusive story listening and reporting are not encouraged or even considered in most homes and schools, where only the verbal message counts.

What children know about a story from its sounds is like a well-kept secret in which children use listening skills that may not know they possess. Gathering information from sound effects, voice and music enhances story listening so much, it deserves to be acknowledged and cultivated. Asking more direct questions, playing games of recognizing or naming music, and matching music to words, pictures, or other sounds, are several ways to help children savor what their listening tells them.,

Listening and reading

Listening to stories an being able to read are related. In many studies, early readers are reported to have heard books read aloud regularly when they were preschoolers. Children's comprehension of spoken language and of written prose also are related; children who understand radio stories better have higher standardized reading scores. Why is learning to read associated with listening to literature?

Listening to language exercises mental skills also needed to read. In both activities, a child must concentrate on the orderly flow of language, identify words, interpret them in grammatical context, and remember their meaning. Such basic abilities help listener and reader alike when it comes to following a story or extracting its main points. If anything , listening tends to bias children's learning toward the gist or essential message of a story, whereas reading leads to batter memory for verbatim derails. There is an added advantage in listening to literary language; because it follows more formal rules of grammar an vocabulary than ordinary conversation, the word patterns children hear listening to fiction approximate those they must deal with when reading.

The younger the child, and the less skilled in reading, the greater the potential payoff from prose listening. But what benefit accrues to listeners once they are fluent readers? Perhaps skilled readers proceeding at their own pace even understand more from a text than do listeners. Speech detracts from a story's effectiveness. Young children have definite preferences for speaking rate and have been found to favor slightly faster speech than older children and adults. In fact, listening an reading skills usually even out with age. College students summarize stories equally well after listening or reading. Admittedly, listening to stories is more luxury than skill developer among able readers, but I recommended making it a luxury you consider necessary.

Listening to stories also expands children's literary universe and may increase their incentive to read. Young listeners can be introduced to literature far beyond their reading level: children entering first grade understand more words than they will learn to red in the first grade understand more words than they will learn to read in the first five years of school. Prior exposure to a tale on record or radio will motivate some children to try reading the book. Audio productions that bring to life worthly characters and situations can stay with a child for life. They did for at least one Broadway playwright:

> I listened to the radio. Shows like 'The Green Hornet' and 'The Lone Ranger' and 'Let's Pretend' appealed to the imagination. I had to make a theater in my head for those shows. I made a little stage for the Metropolitan Opera broadcasts every Saturday. I had little figures of Rigoletto and Aida. I'd move the scenery. To me, that was more real than life. I spent a great deal of time in my room with the door closed-but happy.

Few adults can point so clearly to an early media experience as a source of inspiration for later professional success. And time spent with the unobtrusive radio may be especially elusive to memory. But radio and audio permit a very personal response to storytelling which should not be neglected by children, who are just learning how to listen.

Hands on

Encourage children to listen to stories. It will help them appreciate not only language and literature, but the myriad of sounds that surround them.

What to listen to

Younger children When selecting audio fiction for children, consider both subject matter and production quality. The younger the child, the more important it is to find stories that make ample use of character voices, music and other sounds that help convey narrative meaning. The more well-placed sound cues the better. Not that a six-year -old should never hear prose read. But they will better understand-and perhaps sit still longer for- the fully dramatized story that narration. Remember too that the sound of words has more immediate impact than their meaning. That is why poems, songs, and nursery rhymes make such good listening for young children.

Older children School age listeners who are proficient with language can get more out of highly worded stories. They may especially enjoy language that plays with word sound and meaning, such as tongue twisters, riddles and homonyms. Once we master any symbol system, language being just one, it is fun to experiment with and test its limits.

Familiarity Children's listening is effected by familiarity with a story. It is easier to listen to a story you already know. Then, if you become distracted during the telling, you can more readily retrieve the story's thread and reconstruct the missing piece. Second time listeners are being reminded of a narrative, not first having to learning it. On the other hand, children who hear a story they have already seen on TV, in a movie, or in print, lose the opportunity to picture it first themselves.

When it comes to audio, familiarity with a story refers not only to the text. but to voices, music and other sounds. Hearing stories told by people children know and like adds to their appeal. Tape record yourself reading stories. Children may want to participate in the taping by playing the part of a character or making sound effects. This makes wonderful listening when children are at home by themselves.

When, Where, and how to listen

Locating conducive conditions for story listening is winning half the battle. Consider children's schedules in light of what you know about story listening that it demands concentration, that there is nothing to look at, that other sounds will compete for their attention. Sorry listening suggests quite times and places where children's movement is already restricted . Times spent traveling in the car, for instance, offers ripe occasions for bringing along a battery-powered tape recorder and a few tapes. How about listening to adventures in far-off places in route the supermarket? Passengers can listen together or a child can use earphones and listen alone. Listening to stories also can be a refreshing alternative to watching TV for children home sick in bed. The bathtub makes ideal terrain in which to safely heed the call of sea adventures. A little nook of cranny in the classroom can be outfitted for listening as well.

Occupying eyes and hands is part of the challenge facing listeners. The easiest solution is to listen in the dark. Spooky stories are the best, although children may prefer bearing them with other people around. Once lights are on, however, young listeners may bot be content to just sit and gaze off into space. Another approach is to make materials available for youngsters to look at and handle during a broadcast or recording. They may be related to the narrative, like the storybooks that often accompany records and tapes. These booklets can improve listening comprehension by offering a printed or picture version of the story. But children also like using materials unrelated to a story while they listen. They can elaborate on a story's content as then please with the help of paper, pencils, play figures, clay and building sets. Reversing the emphasis, an audio drama can be used to motivate an art project.

Index